Fiction and Nonfiction

CLEAR Curriculum Units From the University of Virginia
FOR GRADE 4

Fiction and Nonfiction

LANGUAGE ARTS UNITS FOR GIFTED STUDENTS IN GRADE 4

Carolyn M. Callahan, Ph.D.,
Tracy C. Missett, Ph.D.,
Amy Price Azano, Ph.D.,
Melanie Caughey,
Annalissa V. Brodersen, Ph.D.,
& Mary Tackett, Ph.D.

Routledge
Taylor & Francis Group
NEW YORK AND LONDON

First published in 2017 by Prufrock Press Inc.

Published 2021 by Routledge
605 Third Avenue, New York, NY 10017
2 Park Square, Milton Park, Abingdon, Oxon OX14 4RN

Routledge is an imprint of the Taylor & Francis Group, an informa business

Cover and layout design by Raquel Trevino

ISBN 13: 978-1-0321-4429-0 (hbk)
ISBN 13: 978-1-6182-1649-6 (pbk)

DOI: 10.4324/9781003235194

Additional resources can be found at
https://www.routledge.com/9781618216496

TABLE OF CONTENTS

ACKNOWLEDGMENTS

Special credit and acknowledgment must go to the many faculty, researchers, and graduate research assistants who played roles in the development of the CLEAR Curriculum Model; the poetry, research, and folktales units that are included in this series; and the assessments that accompany those units. The CLEAR Curriculum Model was the brainchild of Dr. Catherine Brighton and Dr. Holly Hertberg-Davis. Their original conception of the model led to the drafts of the units mentioned above by then graduate research assistants: Jennifer Beasely, Marla Capper, Jane Jarvis, Maureen Murphy, and Mary Beth Samsa-Hes. Further revisions of the folktale unit were made by Mindy Labernz. Dr. Tonya Moon was a contributor to the development of the performance assessments included in the unit. After field tests and initial implementation of the units by the teachers involved in the study of the units, Dr. Kimberly Landrum worked with the team to further refine the units with the authors of this series. Without each one of them this publication would not have been possible.

And, of course, we must acknowledge the work of Dr. Sandra N. Kaplan, Dr. Joseph S. Renzulli, and Dr. Carol A. Tomlinson, whose foundational work in gifted education guided our thinking in the conceptualization of the model and in the development of units that would challenge and engage gifted learners.

Part I

Introduction and Using the CLEAR Curriculum Units

DOI: 10.4324/9781003235194-1

Introduction

As researchers at the National Research Center on the Gifted and Talented, we recently completed a 6-year study of the effectiveness of two units based on the CLEAR Curriculum Model. The CLEAR (Challenge Leading to Engagement, Achievement, and Results) Curriculum Model incorporates elements from three widely-used, research-based models in gifted education—differentiation, depth and complexity, and the Schoolwide Enrichment Model—by Carol Tomlinson, Sandra Kaplan, and Joseph Renzulli, respectively. The CLEAR Curriculum Model addresses the recognition by leaders in the field that the heart of effective programming for gifted education services lies in the development and the implementation of curricula and instructional strategies that will challenge and enhance learning outcomes for high-ability learners.

The CLEAR Curriculum Model is comprised of five foundational elements:

1. continual formative assessment,
2. clear learning goals,
3. data-driven learning experiences,
4. authentic products, and
5. rich curriculum.

These elements are integrated into a curricular framework that reflects both the language arts Common Core State Standards and the National Association

DOI: 10.4324/9781003235194-2

for Gifted Children Pre-K to Grade 12 Gifted Programming Standards. This integration ensures layers of challenge, opportunities for more in-depth study, and the production of authentic work resembling that of professionals within a discipline.

Teachers who participated in our study implemented two language arts units, one in poetry and one in research, in their third-grade gifted classrooms. The poetry unit, "The Magic of Everyday Things," received the 2012 Curriculum Award from the National Association of Gifted Children. As researchers for the study, we visited more than 100 classrooms across the country and interviewed more than 100 teachers who implemented the CLEAR units. We observed their teaching, their interactions with the curriculum, and student engagement. We also analyzed student achievement data, which indicated that the CLEAR Curriculum works! That is, students who were exposed to the units outperformed peers in gifted classrooms who did not have access to the curriculum.

We also listened to our participating teachers throughout the study. These teachers reported not only that students thrived during the poetry and research units but also that they—the teachers—learned a great deal about best practices in the field of gifted education. Teachers shared that for the first time they finally understood how to differentiate instruction for their students. Buzz phrases like "authentic products" and "formative assessments" came to life, providing a unique source of professional development for teachers whose endorsement credentials vary from state to state. Because no other available curriculum integrates the most popular models of gifted instruction in a way that the CLEAR Curriculum does, these teacher reports provide extraordinary testimony.

Finally, we worked with gifted coordinators who shared their frustrations about the loss of personnel and professional development opportunities vital to the livelihoods of their gifted education programs in the context of a tough economic climate that devalues gifted education programs and the students served in them. We heard their expressed appreciation for the opportunities for professional development embedded within the poetry and research units themselves.

Throughout our research, we fielded countless e-mails and telephone calls from our participating teachers, their principals, and district coordinators and, resoundingly, they asked: *Where can we get more?*

This three-part series answers that question.

CLEAR CURRICULUM UNITS FOR GIFTED STUDENTS (GRADES 3–5)

The CLEAR Curriculum Units for Gifted Students (grades 3–5) offer two units per grade level for a total of six distinct units based on the CLEAR Curriculum Model. All units put theory into practice and provide teachers with research-based curricula. What's more is that these units are based on a tested model that has been shown to work. For more on their effectiveness, see an article in the *American Educational Research Journal*, in which Callahan, Moon, Oh, Azano, and Hailey (2015) presented the achievement data documenting the success of the poetry (grade 3) and research (grade 5) units for students exposed to them.

WHAT IS INCLUDED?

Each book in the series contains two grade-level appropriate language arts units based on the CLEAR Curriculum Model, including the award-winning and empirically supported poetry and research units. Each unit incorporates best practices from the field of gifted education while promoting critical literacy skills for the gifted student. Although each book can stand alone, the units are also vertically aligned so that a student advancing through all three grades can encounter innovative and challenging language arts lessons that have clear scope and sequence of learning outcomes that extend the Common Core State Standards (CCSS).

Let us tell you more about the CLEAR Curriculum Model.

THE CLEAR CURRICULUM MODEL

The CLEAR Curriculum Model is a synthesis of fundamental and compatible curricular features from (a) the Differentiated Instruction Model (Tomlinson, 1995, 1999), (b) the Schoolwide Enrichment Model (SEM; Renzulli & Reis, 1985, 2001); and (c) the Depth and Complexity Model (Kaplan, 2005). The CLEAR Curriculum Model was developed as part of a Jacob K. Javits research grant authored by Carolyn M. Callahan, Tonya R. Moon, Holly Hertberg-Davis, and Catherine M. Brighton.

The Differentiated Instruction Model (Tomlinson, 1995, 1999) aims to address the diverse learning needs of students across differing ability levels, interests, and learning profiles. Its success is grounded in modifying three key elements of curriculum—content, process, and product—based on variations in student learning characteristics. As such, differentiation is a flexible instructional model for a broad range of students, including those who are gifted, based on the incorporation of a variety of both curricular and instructional arrangements. Several concepts from differentiation, as conceptualized in Tomlinson's model, lie at the heart of the CLEAR Curriculum Model. For example, the use of continual formative assessments supports teachers in differentiating the academic experiences included in the curriculum and aids teachers in acting on their recognition that gifted students learn and express learning in unique and diverse ways. More specifically, the continual formative assessments provide valuable feedback, or data, to teachers about individual student readiness and inform "next steps" instruction for diverse gifted learners. Thus, the data derived from continual formative assessments allow for tailoring of the curriculum to each student.

Differentiation is also evident in the flexible grouping arrangements provided in the CLEAR units. The use of flexible grouping arrangements facilitates matching the pace of learning, degree of challenge and interests of students to instructional tasks, and allows students to create individualized products that reflect their learning (Tomlinson, 1995, 1999). Whole-group, small-group, and independent activities simultaneously build community and foster autonomy.

The SEM (see Renzulli & Reis, 1985, 2001) represents one of the most important contributions to the field of gifted education, and SEM has been adopted by many school districts across the county. At its core, SEM stresses the creative process and encourages academic experiences that mirror the work of "real-world" professionals. SEM promotes student engagement through the use of three types of enrichment experiences, which include (a) exposure to extensions of traditional content within the context of its use by real-world professionals (Type I learning experiences), (b) development of process skills that are applied to solving real problems (Type II learning experiences), and (c) investigations of topics and/or creation of products that reflect in-depth investigations into solving real problems in areas of student interest and ability (Type III learning experiences). The feature of SEM that is differentiated at the highest tier is student choice of independent topics for investigation, where students can engage in meaningful learning within the context of real problems in a field and create products demonstrating the skills of an expert in that field. The elements of student choice and authentic investigation are evident throughout the CLEAR units.

The underlying principles of the Depth and Complexity Model (Kaplan, 2005) characterize the CLEAR units and contribute to building layers of challenge and meaning for students. Depth and Complexity employs standards-based curriculum as the basis for promoting academic rigor. The model develops advanced levels of understanding by integrating elements of depth and complexity. To provide depth, CLEAR units focus on big ideas, language of the discipline, details, and patterns, and then those concepts are coupled with a

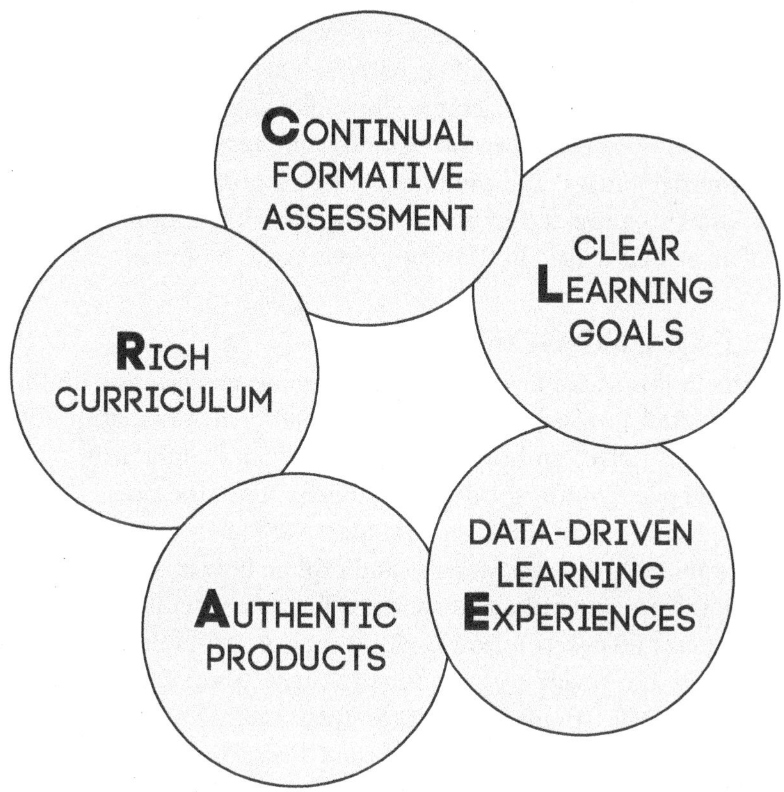

FIGURE 1. THE CLEAR CURRICULUM MODEL.

focus on complexity, including multiple perspectives, interdisciplinary connections, and ethical issues (Kaplan, 2005). The dimension of complexity affords teachers and students multiple opportunities to think deeply about the content and identify associations and relationships that exist within, between, and among areas of study. Accordingly, the CLEAR units are designed to ensure that students recognize that big ideas and principles are rarely simple. Using these elements of the model also allows for the development of critical literacy skills, as students learn how to "read" bias—their own and others.

Based on the compatible theoretical underpinnings of Tomlinson's, Kaplan's, and Renzulli's curriculum models, as well as principles of exemplary curriculum development in general, the units reflect five foundational elements (see Figure 1) evident throughout all of the CLEAR units.

CONTINUAL FORMATIVE ASSESSMENT

The CLEAR units use formative assessments throughout to provide valuable feedback about students to teachers. Formative assessments serve as a guide to planning instruction with student responses to the assessments informing subsequent instruction. Each unit includes both the formative assessment tool as well as thorough instruction on how assessment data from that tool can be used to differentiate lessons. Use of formative assessment in this manner allows teacher flexibility with the curriculum, thus allowing the instruction to meet students where they are in terms of readiness, interests, and learning profiles. Exit cards, journal entries, and multiple choice responses are examples of formative assessments provided to teachers throughout the units. Figure 2 is an example of an exit card used in the fifth-grade research unit.

CLEAR LEARNING GOALS

The units in this series have clear learning goals consistent with the Pre-K to Grade 12 Gifted Programming Standards (National Association for Gifted Children [NAGC], 2010) and the Common Core State Standards (CCSS). For example, in the poetry unit, third-grade students read the poem "The Fish," a poem more advanced than third-grade students are likely to read. Students are asked to determine the central message and explain how it is conveyed through the details in the poem, to distinguish literal from nonliteral language, refer to parts of the poem and describe how each successive part builds on earlier parts, and explain how the poem conveys mood. These components of the poetry unit integrate multiple standards for third grade in the English Language Arts Standards, Reading: Literature strand of the CCSS. However, these standards are applied to more advanced content to address the advanced readiness levels of gifted students. Throughout all units close attention has been paid to basing lessons on both the CCSS and the NAGC standards.

DATA-DRIVEN LEARNING EXPERIENCES

The philosophical principle underlying the CLEAR units is that gifted learners are diverse in their readiness levels and interests and they learn best when their diverse needs are met in the classroom. Consistent with this philosophy, the units include ongoing formative and summative assessments that provide data for teachers to use in effectively differentiating instruction and learning opportunities for students and assessing student learning.

AUTHENTIC PRODUCTS

In keeping with the Schoolwide Enrichment Model, the CLEAR units provide multiple opportunities for students to create authentic products, to develop real-world skills, and to apply knowledge in relevant contexts. These authentic products take the shape of poetry readings, debates, research presentations, letters to the editor, rhetoric (persuasive arts) journals, and so forth. Students not only acquire knowledge but also use the skills and content they have learned as experts in fields such as poetry, research, and fiction writing.

PREPARATION: FORMATIVE ASSESSMENT 3

At the end of Lesson 4, have students respond to the following "Exit Card" in their journals:

Choose either Question 1 or 2 to answer on your card. Everyone must answer Question 3. Please put your name on your card.

1. Before you begin looking for the answers to your research question, what should you do first?
2. What is a *source*?
3. How does what you already know about a topic (your prior knowledge) help you in getting more information about it?

FIGURE 2. SAMPLE "EXIT CARD" FOR FORMATIVE ASSESSMENT.

RICH CURRICULUM

A focus on "big ideas" in the various CLEAR units allows for the achievement of deep understanding. For example, a big idea in the poetry unit is: "Poetry helps readers see the extraordinary (the magic) in the ordinary." A big idea in the research unit is: "Values, experiences, and motivation contribute to the development of an explorer's (reader's) perspective and purpose." In each unit developed using the CLEAR Curriculum Model, students are challenged to question, to investigate, to answer unanswered questions, and then to question what they find. The CLEAR units stress that there are rarely "easy" answers to hard questions—as such, students will sharpen critical literacy skills as they begin to consider varied perspectives and ethical issues within a unit of study.

CRITICAL LITERACY

Literacy skills are no longer limited to the tasks of reading, writing, and speaking. Students are inundated with nonfiction texts and media messages and must have the necessary skills to interpret those messages. Paulo Freire (1970) argued that literacy is always political and redirected the field of literacy instruction to consider social justice and the transformative power of literacy. The CLEAR units will emphasize critical literacy skills, challenging students to consider the political and social implications of the topics and concepts taught. Students are media consumers and must learn to do what Freire (with Macedo, 1987) described as reading the "word" and the "world."

EVIDENCE-BASED PRACTICE

In the current educational environment of accountability, educators, researchers, and policy makers increasingly expect the development and adoption of evidence-based practices, or those that are proven to be effective in raising student achievement. At the same time, a principle contention in the field of gifted education is that gifted students require comprehensive differentiated curricula and instruction to develop their abilities effectively. Thus, the field of gifted education has urged the development and deployment of rigorously conducted curriculum intervention studies to demonstrate that recommended curricula and practices for gifted learners are evidence-based and have demonstrated measurable academic growth for gifted learners.

It was in the context of accountability that the National Research Center on the Gifted and Talented sought to draw from curriculum models with features that had research support and create a new model that could itself demonstrate effectiveness in raising student achievement. As indicated above, the developers of the CLEAR Curriculum Model synthesized components of SEM, differentiation, and depth and complexity that were shown to positively impact student learning outcomes.

Specifically, theoretical support for differentiation comes from learning and development theories that propose (a) optimal learning is achieved when learners are exposed to tasks slightly above their current level of performance (Csikszentmihalyi, 1990; Csikszentmihalyi, Rathunde, & Whalen, 1993; Howard, 1994; Jensen, 1998; Sousa & Tomlinson, 2010) and (b) learning should focus on understanding of key knowledge and principles of the field of study rather than rote memorization of information (e.g., Donovan, Bransford, & Pellegrino, 1999; Wenglinsky, 2002). Studies have documented positive effects of the model in student achievement across subject areas, grades, and performance levels and higher level thinking skills with diverse learners in a variety of school settings. Research on the effectiveness of depth and complexity (cited in Kaplan, 2013) has documented academic growth in social studies and language arts among elementary students at all ability levels including gifted students. The effectiveness of SEM has been shown in raising student creative productivity, student personal and social development, and student self-efficacy (e.g., Burns, 1987; Olenchak, 1991; Reis, 1981; Schack, Starko, & Burns, 1991). Moreover, investigations of SEM as a curricular framework in a reading intervention for elementary students of all ability levels including advanced learners have shown higher scores in reading achievement, reading fluency, and students' attitudes toward reading.

The National Research Center on the Gifted and Talented then investigated the effectiveness of the two language arts units—poetry and research—developed from the CLEAR Curriculum Model. After implementing the work in more than 100 classrooms over a period of 4 years, researchers analyzed observations, interviews, teacher logs, surveys, student products, and student outcomes to conclude that students who were provided instruction with the units earned significantly higher achievement test scores than students in classes where the units were not used. A more detailed report of the impact of the units studied can be found in Callahan et al. (2015). Importantly, these positive results were observed in both full-time inclusive gifted settings and pull-out gifted settings. Because the most prevalent service option for gifted learners is pull-out programs with instructional blocks of 45–60 minutes once or twice a week, the units were designed so the whole unit could be completed during the fall/winter or winter/spring sessions in a typical pull-out classroom, including time for ongoing assessments and the creation of an authentic product for each unit. However, the units are structured so that they can also be used daily in self-contained gifted classrooms or with the frequency deemed appropriate by teachers in that setting. Thus, the CLEAR units can be used in a variety of group and classroom arrangements.

OVERVIEW OF THE BOOKS

These books are for gifted education teachers, gifted education coordinators, and regular education teachers who serve gifted students in their classrooms. Each grade-level book offers two complete units of study. Each unit contains 10–20 lessons designed for 45–60 minute classes. Within the units, content and skills are developed to reflect a clear scope and sequence of learning opportunities. The following outline details the organization of the grade-level units based on the CLEAR Curriculum Model and identifies the relevant Common Core State Standards in English Language Arts addressed and extended in each unit.

GRADE 3 UNITS: POETRY AND FAIRY TALES

LITERACY AND CRITICAL LITERACY SKILLS IN GRADE 3 UNITS

(CCSS.ELA-Literacy.RL.3.1–3.10; CCSS.ELA-Literacy.W 3.3–3.6, 3.10)

- All texts/sources are influenced by author's purpose and perspective
- Information comes from multiple sources
- Understanding bias and cultural contexts
- Informed consumers of information

POETRY

In this unit, students will read and analyze various forms of poetry and write their own poetry anthology. They will learn how to identify and use figurative language to create concrete images from abstract ideas.

FAIRY TALES

In this unit, students will study fairy tales and folklore to understand how and why societal norms and mores are culturally transmitted.

GRADE 4 UNITS: FICTION AND NONFICTION

LITERACY AND CRITICAL LITERACY SKILLS IN GRADE 4 UNITS

(CCSS.ELA-Literacy.RL.4.1–4.10; CCSS.ELA-Literacy.W 4.1–4.10)

- Understanding texts as reflections of culture (politics)
- Understanding informative/explanatory texts contain personal opinions and points of view
- Authors manipulate details
- Readers have filters for information (implicit bias)
- Fiction and nonfiction are equally biased/loaded

FICTION

In this unit, students will read and analyze short stories, develop an understanding of how short story writers develop plot and characters in a concise narrative setting without sacrificing compelling storytelling, and write their own short story.

NONFICTION

In comparison to the fiction (short story) unit, students will study nonfiction (and creative nonfiction) texts to examine how writers use many of the same devices to tell nonfiction stories. Students will read a variety of nonfiction texts and will write their own memoir.

GRADE 5 UNITS: RESEARCH AND RHETORIC

LITERACY AND CRITICAL LITERACY SKILLS IN GRADE 5 UNITS

(CCSS.ELA-Literacy.RL.5.1–5.10; CCSS.ELA-Literacy.W 5.1–5.10; CCSS.ELA-Literacy.SL.5.1–5.4; CCSS.ELA-Literacy.RI.5.1–5.10)

- Creating texts for purpose
- Speakers manipulate audiences
- Yielding and wielding bias
- Understanding the speaker's perspective
- Understanding the audience's perspective

RESEARCH

In this unit, students will learn and employ advanced research skills from crafting open-ended research questions to discerning between reliable sources. Using the Big6 research process, created by Michael B. Eisenberg and Robert E. Berkowitz, students will carry out their own research study and present findings at a research gala.

RHETORIC

Students will engage in a study of Aristotle's *Rhetoric* to answer the question: *When do you appeal to one's intellect, emotions, or sense of morality when trying to persuade?* Students will learn to identify and analyze a variety of rhetorical devices to better understand the art of rhetoric.

Using the CLEAR Curriculum Units

In the introduction, we provided an overview of the three foundational models used in the CLEAR Curriculum Model (Differentiated Instruction Model, Schoolwide Enrichment Model, and the Depth and Complexity Model), the five foundational elements of CLEAR (continual formative assessment, clear learning goals, data-driven learning experiences, authentic products, and rich curriculum), evidence from a multiyear research study, and an overview of the units in this curriculum series. In this section, we offer more specific information about the elements you will find in each unit, including information about how the CLEAR Curriculum Model comes to life in the teaching of these language arts units.

THE SCOPE OF EACH UNIT

Each unit emphasizes "big ideas" within a major focus area in language arts instruction: poetry, storytelling, fiction, nonfiction, rhetoric, and research. Consistent with national standards, these big ideas are then delineated by objectives and vocabulary terms For example, a big idea in the poetry unit is for students to see the extraordinary in the ordinary. For students to grasp that abstract

DOI: 10.4324/9781003235194-3

notion, they must practice reading and writing many forms of poetry. They need to understand how poets use figurative language to render the abstract concrete or the inanimate animate. And they do this while becoming poets—collecting ideas, reading as writers, workshopping their poems, and publishing their work. These big ideas allow teachers and students to concentrate efforts on the "how" and "why" of literacy instruction.

Each unit begins with an overview of the big ideas, learning objectives, and a unit outline that gives an overview of each particular lesson, the related big idea(s), and the targeted skills. The units also begin with a section on "preparing to teach" which provides teachers with information related to resources, materials, classroom environment, classroom management, and ongoing assessments as they relate to that particular unit.

Instruction in each unit is based on a preassessment that is the lead-off activity. Each unit contains several formative assessments that are integrated throughout, and concludes with performance and summative assessments. In each unit, students will produce an authentic product (collection of poems, short story, memoir, speech, etc.). The units also include rubrics for assessing these authentic products.

THE ICONS USED THROUGHOUT THE UNITS

Integrated throughout the lesson plans are a series of icons or symbols intended to draw your attention to the particular content focus, learning objective, or instructional configuration of each learning activity. Some of these icons are derived from Sandra Kaplan's Depth and Complexity Model, while others have been developed specifically for the CLEAR Curriculum Model used in these units. Icons fall into five major categories: Lesson Organization, Literacy Focus, Differentiation, Discipline Exploration, and Subject Analysis. These icons serve as a "quick glance" roadmap to guide instruction. Here we will explain the icons and how they are used throughout the units.

LESSON ORGANIZATION

There are four icons used to indicate how students should be grouped for instructional activities.

Whole-Class Instruction. The teacher leads an activity with the entire class together.

Small-Group Work. Students engage in a learning task in pairs or small groups of 3–5.

Independent Work. Students work on their own in identifying a topic of study, conducting research, and writing or using other modes of expression to present information or demonstrate understanding.

Anchor Activity. As students work at different paces, there will be times when some students finish a task sooner than others. An anchor activity is a task on which students work (usually independently) after they complete other class work. An anchor activity is meaningfully related to the learning objectives of the lesson or unit, allowing students to explore essential ideas, rather than simply a time-filler. All students will have a chance to work on anchor activities over the course of a unit.

LITERACY FOCUS

There are four icons used to indicate the literacy focus of instruction.

Word Study. Students are engaged in learning and practicing how to decode words by breaking them down into their component parts such as sounds, syllables, roots, prefixes, and suffixes. Each student works with words that match his or her own readiness level.

Reading Comprehension. Students are reading for the purpose of understanding and practicing comprehension strategies.

Writing. Students are engaged in one or more stages of the writing process.

Critical Literacy. Students are engaged in thinking about the political and/or social implications of the topics and concepts being taught. They are reading the "word" (text) and the "world" (context).

DIFFERENTIATION

There are four icons to indicate how teachers can differentiate a particular activity.

Differentiation by Readiness. Readiness-based differentiation is the process of adjusting learning experiences to match individual students' levels of past achievement and point of development. Readiness refers to what students already know, understand, and can do related to the learning objectives for a particular task, lesson, or unit. A student's level of readiness might vary depending on his or her background knowledge, prior learning experiences, and profile of competencies related to different topics or kinds of activities. When learning tasks are matched to a student's level of readiness (i.e., within the student's zone of proximal development), the student has the opportunity to work at something that is both challenging and rewarding. When a task is too challenging or not challenging enough for a student, learning is unlikely to occur. Thus, it is essential that general lesson plans be adjusted to better tend to differing levels of readiness among students. Students might work in readiness groups or independently on tasks that are differentiated by readiness.

Differentiation by Interest. Interest-based differentiation refers to the process of adjusting learning experiences to match individual students' interests. When students have the opportunity to work in an area of personal interest to them, they are more likely to become motivated to learn and therefore actively engaged in the learning process. Teachers can attend to students' interests by offering a choice of several materials or topics, by inviting students to suggest their own topics for study, or by allowing students to sometimes work in interest-based groups.

Learning Profile. Learning-profile-based differentiation is the process of adjusting learning experiences to match an individual student's pattern of strengths, weaknesses, and preferences that determines how he or she takes in, makes sense of, and expresses information. Learning profile is shaped by factors such as culture, gender, and learning style preferences. Teachers can provide opportunities for students to work in ways that match their learning profile preferences by incorporating multiple modes of expression and ways of working into the life of the classroom.

Twice-Exceptional Learners. Some students in gifted classrooms also have a disability—such as a specific learning disability, Attention Deficit Hyperactivity Disorder, autism spectrum disorder, and/or an emotional and behavioral disorder—that impedes their ability to learn. These students are commonly referred to as twice-exceptional or "2E" learners. As more students with disabilities are participating in gifted programs, it is important to shift the primary focus of instructional strategies away from remediation and social skills improvement for gifted students with disabilities and toward their strengths, talents, and interests to promote social, emotional, and academic gains, and also to expose these students to rich curricula. The CLEAR language arts units provide a structured model with instructional strategies directed toward developing student strengths (e.g., ability grouping, acceleration, formative assessment) that are recommended for both gifted students and students with disabilities. However, in recognition that these students will sometimes need additional support structures, the 2E icon supports teachers in their use of effective instructional strategies for twice-exceptional students.

DISCIPLINE EXPLORATION

There are five icons used to explain how the discipline can be explored and where the teacher can focus student attention during instructional activities.

Big Idea. A big idea refers to an essential understanding about a topic or discipline that students should take away from the lesson or unit. It often helps to "unpack" or explain an important concept or the relationship between two or more concepts. Big ideas help students move beyond the facts and skills they are learning to focus on what is fundamentally important, enduring, and transferable about the topic. For example, in the poetry unit, students explore the big idea that poetry helps readers see the extraordinary in the ordinary. This is a big idea that guides the work of contemporary poets as they use concrete, sensory language and specific imagery to add layers of meaning to the description of everyday objects, events, and experiences. The big idea can be explored across different poems, poets, and periods of history. In this way, the big idea is a focal point that holds the unit together; students are gradually guided, through a range of learning activities, to arrive at a deep understanding of the big idea. The term *big idea* is sometimes used synonymously with principle, generalization, or understanding.

Place-Based Pedagogy. This task allows students to think critically about how this text (or context) relates to their own sense of place or local community.

Language of the Discipline. The task helps students achieve greater depth of understanding by coming to know and apply the vocabulary of professionals in the academic discipline.

Tools of the Discipline. The task helps students achieve greater depth of understanding by coming to know and apply the ways of thinking and working of professionals in the academic discipline.

Real-World Application. The task requires students to apply the language and tools of the discipline in an environment or activity similar to what an expert in the field would experience.

SUBJECT ANALYSIS

There are three icons used to indicate how a task offers students depth and complexity of a particular topic.

Details. The task helps students achieve greater depth of understanding by studying the essential details relevant to what they are learning.

Patterns. The task helps students achieve greater depth of understanding by analyzing the patterns and trends that can be identified in what they are learning.

Over Time. The task helps students achieve a more complex level of understanding by guiding them to consider what they are learning from a historical perspective.

TIPS

The tip icon indicates an important note for the teacher. The tip might refer to something to watch out for, such as potential classroom management issues or a particular type of talent potential during a learning activity.

ASSESSMENTS IN THE UNITS

There are four types of assessments used throughout the units. Each unit begins with a preassessment to gauge students' initial interest and conceptual knowledge of the unit topic. For example, in poetry students are asked: *What do you know about poetry? What are some of the ways poets make their poems interesting? What would you like to learn about poetry in the next few weeks?* Teachers can use responses to understand students' prior knowledge about the subject and plan subsequent instruction accordingly.

The units also utilize formative assessments throughout. Formative assessments are used to inform next steps in the lesson. Directions are provided on how to use the assessment data to inform instruction in the activities or lessons that follow. For example, in the poetry unit, students take a poetry survey as a formative assessment after Lesson 5. Additionally, teachers are provided with the following instructions for utilizing the data:

> Use information from the assessment to determine whether there is any content you have taught so far that you need to review or reinforce. For example, you might find a group of students having trouble remembering the definition of an adjective or confusing concrete and abstract nouns, and you can plan to take these students aside for a "mini-lesson" at a convenient time. Students' responses to questions about what they would still like to learn might help you choose resources and try to incorporate opportunities to address students' individual interests in later lessons.

Other formative assessments might provide instructions for making decisions about how to group students.

The units also utilize performance and summative assessments. Students will be asked to produce authentic products throughout each of the units, and these final assessments will provide an opportunity for teachers and students to assess learning. For example, the poetry unit ends with a poetry reading and a collection of original works, along with a review of a canonical poem.

GETTING STARTED

The lessons within each unit are clearly marked, along with the assessments, and icons will further direct your instruction. The two units for each grade level can be taught in whichever order you prefer. We hope you and your students enjoy these CLEAR Curriculum units.

Part II

Unit Plans

DOI: 10.4324/9781003235194-4

Unit 1
Finding Your Place in Fiction

BACKGROUND

Finding Your Place in Fiction is a curriculum unit designed to familiarize students with a variety of fictional narratives and to expand their understanding and comprehension of fiction through close examination of story elements, devices, and structure. Through the activities in this unit, students will gain conceptual knowledge of the elements of fiction in order to craft, organize, and write their own narratives. Additionally, students will develop a sense of themselves as critical consumers and producers of fiction as they focus on close reading and analysis of fictional texts.

Students will use their knowledge to create their own narratives with a focus on structuring their writing based on the purpose of their stories. Students will learn how writing structure and choice of language cohesively appeal to the reader's senses, emotions, and images in order to communicate a message or moral about life and to evoke strong emotional connections from the reader. Students will examine how word choice, language, and writing devices can be used to craft compelling stories, and how characters, conflict, and story elements provide opportunities for multiple perspectives and exploration of messages and themes.

DOI: 10.4324/9781003235194-5

Students will also construct characters, conflicts, and plots that suit their individual levels of creativity, interest, and need for challenge. Students will engage in the professional writing process, and will produce an authentic product after carefully prewriting, drafting, revising, editing, and publishing their story in a series of writing workshops. At the completion of the unit, each student will act as a professional in the field, sharing his or her fictional narrative with an audience of students, parents, and teachers at a classroom Author Event and publishing their stories in a Class Anthology.

OBJECTIVES/STANDARDS

This unit is designed to be consistent with common state fourth-grade reading and writing standards, and national standards outlined by the National Council of Teachers of English (NCTE; National Council of Teachers of English & International Reading Association, 2012). It also aligns to the fourth-grade Common Core State Standards (CCSS; an alignment chart is provided on p. 259). This unit addresses the following objectives:

STUDENTS WILL KNOW THE FOLLOWING TERMS

- *Audience* is the group of people for whom an author's writing is intended.
- *Character* is a person, animal, or thing with a personality that appears in a story.
- *Stock characters* are types of characters that are regularly used in fiction.
- *Stereotype* is a character that is simple, usually described with one or two words.
- *Protagonist* is the leading character, hero, or heroine of a literary work.
- *Antagonist* is the principal character in opposition to the protagonist.
- *Characterization* is the act or process of creating a character.
    - *Direct characterization* is where the reader is told what the character is like.
    - *Indirect characterization* occurs when then writer uses details to describe a character.

- *Conflict* addresses incompatibility or disagreement between people or things, particularly those that affect the plot.
    - *Internal conflict* is the psychological struggle within the mind of a literary character that drives the plot.
    - *External conflict* is the struggle between a literary character and an outside force such as nature or another character that drive the plot.

- *Dialogue* is a conversation between two or more people in a story.
- *Genre* is a category of a literary work.
- *Fiction* is a form of literature and involves a story that is invented by the author.
- *Literature* is comprised of written works that generally express universal ideas.
- *Motif* is an important event or thing that occurs over and over in a story.
- *Plot* is the plan or main storyline of a literary work.
- *Point of view* is the perspective from which something is told or considered.
    - *First-person point of view* is a form of storytelling from the perspective of a character writing or speaking directly about him- or herself.
    - *Second-person point of view* is a form of storytelling from the perspective of a narrative onlooker who is writing about you, the reader.
    - *Third-person point of view* is a form of storytelling in which a narrator relates all action in the story using third-person pronouns, such as "he" or "she."
- *Sensory details* relate to sight, hearing, taste, touch, and smell and are used by writers to make the setting come alive.
- *Setting* is used in fiction to identify and establish the time and place of the events of the story.
- *Symbol* is an object, character, figure, or color used to represent an abstract idea or concept.
- *Universal themes* reflect common human experiences that are shared by and appeal to most readers.

STUDENTS WILL UNDERSTAND THE FOLLOWING BIG IDEAS ABOUT FICTION

- Literature is based on universal themes/characters/situations that embody the human experience and help us make sense of our own lives.
- Writers create stories to document and make sense of thoughts/feelings/understandings about themselves and the world around them.
- Writers use senses, emotions, and images to evoke connections between the text and the reader.
- Different perspectives and opinions of an event are legitimate when justified by evidence.

STUDENTS WILL DEMONSTRATE THE FOLLOWING SKILLS

- Use evidence from text to support opinions.
- Make personal connections to fictional narratives.
- Draw conclusions/make inferences about text.
- Recognize different forms of conflict in a fictional narrative.
- Identify the narrator and point of view from which a fictional narrative is told.
- Identify the elements of story structure in a fictional narrative.
- Identify different characteristics in a fictional narrative.
- Identify the structure of a fictional narrative using specific examples from the text.
- Identify and use the elements of a published work of fiction, including the story itself, cover, title page, dedication, and biography.
- Identify different characteristics in a fictional narrative in order to categorize the story by genre.
- Use brainstorming to generate ideas.
- Use descriptive language appropriately.
- Use brainstorming to generate ideas at the prewriting stage of composition.
- Respond to a variety of prompts creatively and thoughtfully.
- Offer constructive criticism both verbally and in writing.
- Write a fictional narrative focusing on a single topic.
- Identify and use different story devices to enrich narrative writing.
- Engage the reader with sentence and word variety.
- Use analysis skills to organize thoughts through prewriting.
- Identify specific steps commonly used in the writing process including prewriting, drafting, editing, revising, and publishing.
- Use different story devices to enrich narrative writing.
- Engage the reader with sentence and word variety.
- Demonstrate knowledge of the fiction genre by writing and presenting an original fictional narrative.
- Use different story devices to enrich narrative writing.
- Demonstrate knowledge of the fiction genre by writing and presenting an original fictional narrative.
- Produce and submit a final fictional narrative for publication using the elements of a story, including the cover, title page, dedication, and biography.

UNIT OUTLINE

	Big Idea(s)	Overview	Skills
Unit Preassessment			
Lesson 1	➢ Writers use senses, emotions, and images to evoke connections between the text and the reader. ➢ Literature is based on universal themes/characters/situations that embody the human experience and help us make sense of our own lives.	*Welcome to Fiction* ➢ Introduction to fiction and the role of sensory imagery in writing.	➢ Use evidence from text to support opinions. ➢ Use brainstorming to generate ideas.
Lesson 2	➢ Writers use senses, emotions, and images to evoke connections between the text and the reader.	*Setting* ➢ The role of sensory imagery. ➢ Introduce setting. ➢ Writing workshop.	➢ Use evidence from text to support opinions ➢ Make personal connections to fictional narratives ➢ Respond to a prompt creatively and thoughtfully ➢ Use descriptive language appropriately
Lesson 3	➢ Writers create stories to document and make sense of thoughts/feelings/understandings about themselves and the world around them. ➢ Writers use senses, emotions, and images to evoke connections between the text and the reader.	*Setting, Continued* ➢ Connect students to their own setting. ➢ Writing workshop.	➢ Respond to a variety of prompts creatively and thoughtfully. ➢ Offer constructive criticism both verbally and in writing. ➢ Write a fictional narrative focusing on a single topic.
Formative Assessment 1			
Lesson 4	➢ Literature is based on universal themes/characters/situations that embody the human experience and help us make sense of our own lives.	*Characters* ➢ Different types of characters.	➢ Read and demonstrate comprehension of fictional texts. ➢ Draw conclusions/make inferences about text.
Lesson 5	➢ Literature is based on universal themes/characters/situations that embody the human experience and help us make sense of our own lives. ➢ Writers use senses, emotions, and images to evoke connections between the text and the reader.	*Characterization* ➢ Review character types. ➢ Introduce characterization. ➢ Writing workshop.	➢ Use brainstorming to generate ideas at the prewriting stage of composition. ➢ Identify and use different story devices to enrich narrative writing. ➢ Identify different characteristics in a fictional narrative.

	Big Idea(s)	Overview	Skills
Lesson 6	⪢ Writers use senses, emotions, and images to evoke connections between the text and the reader. ⪢ Different perspectives and opinions of an event are legitimate when justified by evidence.	*Dialogue* ⪢ How dialogue works in fiction.	⪢ Identify the elements of story structure in a fictional narrative. ⪢ Identify the structure of a fictional narrative using specific examples from the text. ⪢ Identify and use different types of sentences to enhance a narrative/story. ⪢ Engage the reader with sentence and word variety.
Formative Assessment 2			
Lesson 7	⪢ Literature is based on universal themes/characters/situations that embody the human experience and help us make sense of our own lives. ⪢ Writers create stories to document and make sense of thoughts/feelings/understandings about themselves and the world around them. ⪢ Different perspectives and opinions of an event are legitimate when justified by evidence.	*Point of View* ⪢ Writing workshop. ⪢ First- and second-person point of view.	⪢ Identify the narrator and point of view from which a fictional narrative is told ⪢ Respond to a variety of prompts creatively and thoughtfully ⪢ Offer constructive criticism both verbally and in writing
Lesson 8	⪢ Literature is based on universal themes/characters/situations that embody the human experience and help us make sense of our own lives. ⪢ Writers create stories to document and make sense of thoughts/feelings/understandings about themselves and the world around them. ⪢ Different perspectives and opinions of an event are legitimate when justified by evidence.	*Point of View, Continued* ⪢ Writing workshop. ⪢ Third-person point of view and the omniscient and limited narrator.	⪢ Identify the narrator and point of view from which a fictional narrative is told. ⪢ Respond to a variety of prompts creatively and thoughtfully. ⪢ Offer constructive criticism both verbally and in writing.
Lesson 9	⪢ Literature is based on universal themes/characters/situations that embody the human experience and help us make sense of our own lives. ⪢ Different perspectives and opinions of an event are legitimate when justified by evidence.	*Conflict* ⪢ Writing workshop. ⪢ The purpose and role of conflict in fiction.	⪢ Recognize different forms of conflict in a fictional narrative. ⪢ Identify the narrator and point of view from which a fictional narrative is told.

	Big Idea(s)	Overview	Skills
Lesson 10	≫ Writers use senses, emotions, and images to evoke connections between the text and the reader. ≫ Different perspectives and opinions of an event are legitimate when justified by evidence.	*Audience* ≫ Writing workshop. ≫ How audience impacts fiction writing.	≫ Respond to a variety of prompts creatively and thoughtfully. ≫ Offer constructive criticism both verbally and in writing.
Formative Assessment 3			
Lesson 11	≫ Literature is based on universal themes/characters/situations that embody the human experience and help us make sense of our own lives.	*Plot* ≫ Writing workshop. ≫ The nuances of plot structure.	≫ Use brainstorming to generate ideas at the prewriting stage of composition. ≫ Use analysis skills to organize thoughts through prewriting. ≫ Identify specific steps commonly used in the writing process including prewriting, drafting, editing, revising, and publishing.
Lesson 12	≫ Writers use senses, emotions, and images to evoke connections between the text and the reader. ≫ Different perspectives and opinions of an event are legitimate when justified by evidence.	*Openings* ≫ Writing workshop. ≫ The construction of an effective opening in a story.	≫ Use different story devices to enrich narrative writing. ≫ Engage the reader with sentence and word variety. ≫ Demonstrate knowledge of the fiction genre by writing and presenting an original fictional narrative.
Lesson 13	≫ Writers create stories to document and make sense of thoughts/feelings/understandings about themselves and the world around them. ≫ Writers use senses, emotions, and images to evoke connections between the text and the reader.	*Published Works and Genres* ≫ Elements of published works. ≫ Explore genre.	≫ Identify and use the elements of a published work of fiction, including the story itself, cover, title page, dedication, and biography. ≫ Identify different characteristics in a fictional narrative in order to categorize the story by genre. ≫ Use different story devices to enrich narrative writing. ≫ Demonstrate knowledge of the fiction genre by writing and presenting an original fictional narrative. ≫ Produce and submit a final fictional narrative for publication using the elements of a story, including the cover, title page, dedication, and biography.

	Big Idea(s)	Overview	Skills
Lesson 14	➢ Writers create stories to document and make sense of thoughts/feelings/understandings about themselves and the world around them. ➢ Writers use senses, emotions, and images to evoke connections between the text and the reader.	*Writing Workshop: Final Story* ➢ Drafting, revision, and writing.	➢ Use different story devices to enrich narrative writing. ➢ Engage the reader with sentence and word variety. ➢ Demonstrate knowledge of the fiction genre by writing and presenting an original fictional narrative. ➢ Identify the elements of story structure in a fictional narrative. ➢ Recognize different forms of conflict in a fictional narrative. ➢ Use evidence from text to support opinions.
Lesson 15	➢ Writers create stories to document and make sense of thoughts/feelings/understandings about themselves and the world around them. ➢ Writers use senses, emotions, and images to evoke connections between the text and the reader.	*Publication and Author Event*	➢ Use different story devices to enrich narrative writing. ➢ Engage the reader with sentence and word variety. ➢ Demonstrate knowledge of the fiction genre by writing and presenting an original fictional narrative. ➢ Identify the elements of story structure in a fictional narrative. ➢ Recognize different forms of conflict in a fictional narrative. ➢ Use evidence from text to support opinions.
Summative Assessment			

PREPARING TO TEACH THE UNIT

RESOURCES AND MATERIALS

Throughout the unit, the teacher will be reading aloud a variety of narratives that represent different fictional genres. Some of these texts are written above student reading levels but contain sophisticated themes and messages conducive for close analysis that prepares students for thoughtful discussion. Additionally, each story provides an exemplar for the lesson's focus. Links to web-based lesson materials are provided in each lesson plan and on the book's webpage at https://www.routledge.com/9781618216496.

One of the big ideas of this unit is that fictional narratives can evoke strong emotions and connections within the reader. Therefore, while you read aloud, encourage students to enjoy and aesthetically connect with the story they are hearing, to experience and articulate emotions (enjoyment, anticipation, fear, etc.), and to identify the story's structure, language, and themes.

Take the time to help students set up and organize workshop folders at the beginning of the unit to eliminate confusion or the loss of important papers and documents. Workshop folders are pocket folders used to organize a student's work over the course of the unit.

Writer's notebooks can be a composition notebook, journal, spiral bound notebook, etc. Any notebook with lined paper will do.

CLASSROOM ENVIRONMENT

A classroom that allows movement to create a structure that is conducive to whole-class read alouds, group collaboration, and independent work will best serve the teacher and students in this unit. Here are some other tips to help you execute a successful unit:

- Carefully model expectations for daily lesson activities, such as constructive feedback during writers' retreats.
- Identify a prominent place in the classroom for a word wall where important vocabulary and terms can be displayed as students encounter them in the unit.
- Consider also providing a space where students can submit complete Fiction Fanatic Card (Handout 1.4), and a display area similar to the word wall where student examples of the unit vocabulary can be displayed and built upon throughout the unit.

CLASSROOM MANAGEMENT

The success of writing workshop portions of this unit is related to the classroom management of the teacher. During writing workshops, the teacher will monitor the progress of the class as a whole, while also assisting struggling students and challenging more advanced students. During writers' retreats, the teacher will make sure students are offering constructive feedback. The key is to monitor the learning progress of all writers. Consider the following suggestions:

- Use strategies to monitor the progress of the whole class during instructional time (e.g., have students close their workshop folders when ready to share their work).
- Use strategies to identify and assist struggling students without disrupting others who are working independently (e.g., have students display a red slip of paper or a red cup to show they are struggling).

- Ensure that all student writing materials are organized in students' workshop folders so that drafts and writing products are in a safe place and are not mislaid or lost.
- Designate areas of the room for independent writing, teacher conferences, and collaboration, with writing materials organized for easy accessibility.
- At the end of each lesson, remind students to fill out a Fiction Fanatic Card.
- Collect students' workshop folders regularly. This will enable you to keep a current record of student progress and will provide the opportunity to give students specific feedback on their writing.
- When transitioning to writing final stories, prominently display the steps of the writing process that students will move through. Encourage students to monitor their own progress.

ONGOING ASSESSMENT

Administer the unit preassessment to students prior to the first lesson. The purposes of the preassessment are (1) to assess what students already know about the purpose and structure of fictional texts, which will help tailor the activities and group students appropriately, and (2) to provide a baseline for comparison so that the teacher can assess the growth of each student throughout the course of the unit and at the end of the unit.

Administer the formative assessments to students throughout the unit in order to (1) assess students' developing skills so that resources and activities can be tailored to each student and (2) assess what students already know about those aspects of fiction which have been taught or will be taught, which will help tailor the activities and allow teachers to group students appropriately.

There is a summative assessment for this unit—the final story assignment (see Lesson 12). This final assessment is the culminating project, which will result in the Author Event. Students' final products serve as the evidence of their learning, and the accompanying rubric serves as the evaluation tool.

THE CLEAR CURRICULUM MODEL

This unit has been designed using the CLEAR Curriculum Model. The CLEAR (Challenge Leading to Engagement, Achievement, and Results) Curriculum incorporates elements from three research-based curriculum models—differentiation, depth and complexity, and the Schoolwide Enrichment Model—by Carol Tomlinson, Sandra Kaplan, and Joseph Renzulli, respectively. These elements are applied to a curriculum framework that is consistent with state and national standards in reading, but builds layers of challenge and opportunities for more in-depth study authentic to the work of professionals within a discipline, to better meet the needs of all students. Refer to p. 15 for more information about the CLEAR Curriculum Model.

ICONS EXPLAINED

Integrated throughout the lesson plans are a series of icons or symbols intended to draw your attention to the particular content focus, learning objective, or instructional configuration of each learning activity. Some of these icons are derived from Sandra Kaplan's Depth and Complexity curriculum model, while others have been developed specifically for the CLEAR Curriculum Model used in these units. Refer to p. 16 for an explanation of each icon.

LESSON

1 Welcome to Fiction

MATERIALS

- ✓ Student writer's notebooks
- ✓ Teacher's access to excerpt from Chapter 1 of *Alice's Adventures in Wonderland* by Lewis Carroll (available at https://www.gutenberg.org/files/11/11-h/11-h.htm)
- ✓ Handout 1.1: Unit Preassessment
- ✓ Handout 1.2A: Background Activity
- ✓ Handout 1.2B: Background Activity
- ✓ Handout 1.2C: Background Activity
- ✓ Handout 1.3: Sensory Imagery
- ✓ Handout 1.4: Fiction Fanatic Card

Writers use senses, emotions, and images to evoke connections between the text and the reader.

OBJECTIVES

Students will:

- ✓ use evidence from text to support opinions, and
- ✓ use brainstorming to generate ideas.

- Fiction
- Literature
- Universal
- Symbol

SEQUENCE

UNIT PREASSESSMENT

1. Administer the Unit Preassessment (Handout 1.1). Explain to students that this assessment is not for a grade. Rather, it is to find out how much they already know about fiction.

WARM UP

2. Explain to students that they will spend the next few weeks reading and writing fiction. Write *fiction* on the board, and ask students what they think the word *fiction* means.
3. Write down students' responses, and use their phrasing to create a class definition of the term. Students should understand that fiction is invented, imagined, and/or not true. Add *fiction* to the word wall.
4. Explain to students that fiction is a form of literature. Work with students to define *literature* in the same manner as *fiction*. Students should understand that literature is written down and expresses universal ideas. Something universal occurs over and over again, because it is something that is shared among many people. Add *literature* to the word wall.

> Throughout the unit, let students talk about any kinds of fiction that interests them—whether it is books, movies, TV shows, video games, comics, etc.

ACTIVITY: UNIVERSAL ELEMENTS AND AUDIENCE

Read the following statements aloud. If students think it is a universal situation, that it is something that happens everywhere to all people, they should give it a thumbs up. If it is *not* universal, they should give it a thumbs down:

- People are scared of the dark.
- It snows in winter.
- It rains in the spring.
- People get thirsty.
- Schools have drinking fountains.

5. Explain to students that authors use *universal elements* in their stories so that they can appeal to all readers. There are things that may seem universal to students, like having drinking fountains, because it is true for all the schools that they have seen. However, schools in countries like Africa may not have running water. This means it is not true for everyone. However, being thirsty is a feeling that everyone experiences. Therefore, if students read a story about a broken drinking fountain, being thirsty because of it would be universal. Add *universal* to the word wall.

REVIEW: TERMINOLOGY

6. Based on the results of the preassessment, sort students into three readiness groups. Use the levels as needed. You may not have enough students in each category to require three groups.
   - **Group A** (0–3 questions correct on the preassessment) will use Handout 1.2A: Background Activity to match terms, definitions, and examples.
   - **Group B** (4–7 questions correct) will use Handout 1.2B: Background Activity to write in the term for each definition and create their own examples.
   - **Group C** (8–10 questions correct) will use Handout 1.2C: Background Activity to write a definition for each term and create their own examples.

Briefly review the terms on the review activity as a class before moving forward.

APPLICATION: IMAGERY

7. Invite students to find a comfortable place for listening. You will be reading a passage from *Alice's Adventures in Wonderland* by Lewis Carroll. Actually named Charles Dodgson, Carroll stammered when he talked and felt more comfortable when speaking with children. The Alice books were inspired by Alice Liddell, who enjoyed the stories Carroll told her and asked him to write them down. Tell students to enjoy the way the passage sounds but to listen for sensory imagery.
8. Read aloud an excerpt from Chapter 1 (para. 16–17, "It was all very well to say 'Drink me'. . ." through "she very soon finished off.")
9. Ask students: *What kind of sensory imagery does Lewis Carroll use in this passage? How does it help us understand what Alice is experiencing?* Record students' examples.
10. Ask: *When you heard about the bottle being marked "poison," did you get an image in your head?* Have students share what images they may have envisioned. (Students may visualize a skull and crossbones, Mr. Yuk, etc.)
11. Explain that this is an example of a *symbol,* which is an object, character, figure, or color used to represent an abstract idea or concept. Sometimes imagery can have symbolic meanings, so students should keep this in mind when they read. Add *symbol* to the word wall.

Students should note taste and touch, but see if they can justify any other examples of imagery with support from the text.

If you did not have three groups for the activity earlier, divide your students as evenly as possible. Consider asking your students about how they feel about imagery (thumbs up—confident; thumb sideways—okay; thumb down—not sure) and using that for grouping (confident—3; okay—2; not sure—1).

ACTIVITY: SEARCHING FOR SENSORY IMAGERY

12. Distribute Handout 1.3: Sensory Imagery. Divide students into their readiness groups (Group A should read Passage 1, Group B should read Passage 2, etc.). Or consider selecting one (or all) of the passages for the entire class to read. Students should underline any sensory imagery that they find and label the sense. They should also put a star next to any potential symbols. They will share their examples of sensory imagery with the class.

Students can read and think about their group's passage independently if they prefer and then come back to their group to share what they came up with.

13. Assist any students who are having difficulty. When you see that all groups have at least one example, ask them to choose which example to share.
14. Have each group present its example. See if the rest of the class agrees, and if they do not, work through the example until everyone understands. Discuss any symbols students note as well (such as the golden crown—wealth, royalty—in Passage 3).

APPLICATION: FICTION FANATIC

15. Ask: *How many of you read or watch fiction outside of school?* Hopefully, all students will raise their hands! Tell students that to ensure they understand the terminology in this unit, the class will collect as many examples of fictional elements as possible. Students will regularly contribute to the Fiction Fanatic board.
16. Distribute Handout 1.4: Fiction Fanatic Card. In this lesson, students will use the cards to recall sensory imagery or symbols in books, movies, games, TV shows, comics, or other fictional mediums that they enjoy. Demonstrate how to complete a card based on something students have read in class or something that they are all familiar with (e.g., *Frozen* or *Star Wars*). Have students complete a card or turn it in during the next lesson.

- This is a great activity for students who may finish work early, although you should encourage all students to complete these cards, as it will allow you to assess their understanding of the terminology. Make sure you keep extra copies of Handout 1.4: Fiction Fanatic Card accessible so that students can complete them whenever they want to add to the board.
- If possible, also keep a cart of library books in the room for students to generate ideas from in case there are days where students do not have any ideas to bring in from home.

PREPARATION: FOR NEXT LESSON

17. During this unit, students will be working toward becoming authors. Good authors have to practice. Thus, students will take part in various writing workshops. Say: *At the start of each writing workshop, I will start you off by giving you a prompt—a brief paragraph, a sentence, or sometimes just a word—to get you started. Sometimes you might not finish the assignments in class because it can be hard to write on a schedule. You will receive a writer's notebook to keep with you, so you can write down your thoughts during workshop time and any time you want to write at home. At the end of a writing workshop, you will record the response you want to share with the class on a separate sheet of paper. We will read our work out loud and offer constructive criticism to one another during writers' retreats.*
18. Display the following prompt, and read it out loud: *Choose one of the five senses. In approximately 100 words, describe what you had for lunch today (or yesterday) using the sense you have chosen.*
19. Distribute writer's notebooks (see p. 33). Students should begin prewriting, showing how they feel about what they had for lunch—but not telling. Give students the rest of the lesson to work on this, and remind them that it is okay if they need to work on it more at home. They will share their final response during the next lesson.

Explain the difference between a nonconstructive ("I think the description of what Alice drinks is confusing") and a constructive comment ("I think the description of what Alice drinks could be improved if the author added details about how it smelled"). The comments students offer should always offer an opinion about how the author can construct a better story.

HANDOUT 1.1

UNIT PREASSESSMENT

Directions: Fill in each blank with the appropriate word. Then, answer the questions that follow as best as you can.

1. ____________________ is figurative language that gives nonhumans human traits.
2. ____________________ is the feeling people have toward characters when they have experienced something similar.
3. ____________________ are recurring elements that are used to help construct stories.
4. ____________________ are formulaic/oversimplified characters or concepts.
5. What does imagery help us to express?
6. What are some of the reasons that authors write?
7. What is the difference between a *simile* and a *metaphor*? What are examples of each?
8. What is the difference between *abstract* and *concrete language*? What are examples of each?

HANDOUT 1.2A

BACKGROUND ACTIVITY

Directions: Write the correct term to the left of the definition. To the right of the definition, write the letter of the example that you think best fits the definition.

Terms	Examples
Abstract	A. Aesop's fables have a moral to inform the audience about how they should behave.
Concrete	B. Feeling sad when someone drops their ice cream because you get sad when you drop yours.
Empathy	C. Princesses are beautiful and kind.
Imagery	D. Characters who fall into a magical sleep.
Metaphor	E. Anger, courage, fear.
Motif	F. Fence, chicken, boat.
Personification	G. Time flies.
Purpose	H. Life is a highway.
Simile	I. Busy as a bee.
Stereotype	J. Scent of hay on a summer afternoon.

Term		Example
1. ______________	Figurative language that gives nonhumans human traits.	______
2. ______________	The feeling people have toward characters when they have experienced something similar.	______
3. ______________	Recurring elements used to help construct stories.	______

HANDOUT 1.2A, CONTINUED

	Term		Example
4.	____________	Formulaic/oversimplified characters or concepts.	______
5.	____________	Expresses sensory details (sight, sound, touch, taste, smell).	______
6.	____________	Why an author writes, often to inform, entertain, or persuade.	______
7.	____________	Compares two unlike things.	______
8.	____________	Compares two unlike things, using "like". or "as."	______
9.	____________	Lacks physical details.	______
10.	____________	Uses physical details.	______

HANDOUT 1.2B

BACKGROUND ACTIVITY

Directions: Write the correct term to the left of the definition. Underneath the definition, write an example.

TERMS

Abstract	Motif
Concrete	Personification
Empathy	Purpose
Imagery	Simile
Metaphor	Stereotype

	Term	Definition and Example
1.	____________	Figurative language that gives nonhumans human traits. ______________________________ ______________________________
2.	____________	The feeling people have toward characters when they have experienced something similar. ______________________________ ______________________________
3.	____________	Recurring elements that are used to help construct stories. ______________________________ ______________________________
4.	____________	Formulaic/oversimplified characters or concepts. ______________________________ ______________________________

HANDOUT 1.2B, CONTINUED

	Term	Definition and Example
5.	____________	Expresses sensory details (sight, sound, touch, taste, smell). ____________ ____________
6.	____________	Why an author writes, often to inform, entertain, or persuade. ____________ ____________
7.	____________	Compares two unlike things. ____________ ____________
8.	____________	Compares two unlike things, using "like" or "as." ____________ ____________
9.	____________	Lacks physical details. ____________ ____________
10.	____________	Uses physical details. ____________ ____________

Name: ______________________ Date: ______________

HANDOUT 1.2C

BACKGROUND ACTIVITY

Directions: In the left column, write out the definition in your own words. In the right column, write an example.

Definition	Term	Example
	Abstract	
	Concrete	
	Empathy	
	Imagery	
	Metaphor	
	Motif	
	Personification	
	Purpose	
	Simile	
	Stereotype	

HANDOUT 1.3

SENSORY IMAGERY

Directions: Read the following passages. Underline any sensory imagery that you find and label which of the five senses it depicts. Be prepared to share an example with the class.

PASSAGE 1

CHAPTER 1, *ALICE'S ADVENTURES IN WONDERLAND* BY LEWIS CARROLL

Alice opened the door and found that it led into a small passage, not much larger than a rat-hole: she knelt down and looked along the passage into the loveliest garden you ever saw. How she longed to get out of that dark hall, and wander about among those beds of bright flowers and those cool fountains, but she could not even get her head through the doorway; 'and even if my head would go through,' thought poor Alice, 'it would be of very little use without my shoulders. Oh, how I wish I could shut up like a telescope! I think I could, if I only know how to begin.' For, you see, so many out-of-the-way things had happened lately, that Alice had begun to think that very few things indeed were really impossible.

PASSAGE 2

CHAPTER 12, *ALICE'S ADVENTURES IN WONDERLAND* BY LEWIS CARROLL

The long grass rustled at her feet as the White Rabbit hurried by—the frightened Mouse splashed his way through the neighbouring pool—she could hear the rattle of the teacups as the March Hare and his friends shared their never-ending meal, and the shrill voice of the Queen ordering off her unfortunate guests to execution—once more the pig-baby was sneezing on the Duchess's knee, while plates and dishes crashed around it—once more the shriek of the Gryphon, the squeaking of the Lizard's slate-pencil, and

HANDOUT 1.3, CONTINUED

the choking of the suppressed guinea-pigs, filled the air, mixed up with the distant sobs of the miserable Mock Turtle.

So she sat on, with closed eyes, and half believed herself in Wonderland, though she knew she had but to open them again, and all would change to dull reality—the grass would be only rustling in the wind, and the pool rippling to the waving of the reeds—the rattling teacups would change to tinkling sheep-bells, and the Queen's shrill cries to the voice of the shepherd boy—and the sneeze of the baby, the shriek of the Gryphon, and all the other queer noises, would change (she knew) to the confused clamour of the busy farm-yard—while the lowing of the cattle in the distance would take the place of the Mock Turtle's heavy sobs.

PASSAGE 3

CHAPTER 8, *THROUGH THE LOOKING GLASS* BY LEWIS CARROLL

'I hope it encouraged him,' she said, as she turned to run down the hill: 'and now for the last brook, and to be a Queen! How grand it sounds!' A very few steps brought her to the edge of the brook. 'The Eighth Square at last!' she cried as she bounded across, and threw herself down to rest on a lawn as soft as moss, with little flower-beds dotted about it here and there. 'Oh, how glad I am to get here! And what *is* this on my head?' she exclaimed in a tone of dismay, as she put her hands up to something very heavy, and fitted tight all round her head.

'But how *can* it have got there without my knowing it?' she said to herself, as she lifted it off, and set it on her lap to make out what it could possibly be.

It was a golden crown.

 Name: ______________________________ **Date:** ______________

HANDOUT 1.4

FICTION FANATIC CARD

Directions: Write the topic you have been discussing in class at the top of the page. Then, think about an example of the topic that you recall from books, movies, games, TV, comics, or something else that you enjoy. Write down the title and author (if one exists). Describe the example on the pages of the book below. Be as specific as possible!

FICTION FANATIC CARD

Topic: ____

Title: ______________________ Author: ______________________

LESSON 2 Setting

MATERIALS

- ✓ Student writer's notebooks
- ✓ Student workshop folders
- ✓ Teacher's copy of Chapter 1 (pp. 5–6, para. 1–6) from *A Tree Grows In Brooklyn* by Betty Smith (First Harper Perennial Modern Classics Edition, 2005; also available at http://www.npr.org/books/titles/138257002/a-tree-grows-in-brooklyn#excerpt)
- ✓ Handout 1.4: Fiction Fanatic Card
- ✓ Handout 2.1: Writing Workshop Guidelines
- ✓ Appendix A1: Road to Publishing: Imagery and Setting

Writers use senses, emotions, and images to evoke connections between the text and the reader.

OBJECTIVES

Students will:

- ✓ use evidence from text to support opinions,
- ✓ make personal connections to fictional narratives,
- ✓ respond to a prompt creatively and thoughtfully, and
- ✓ use descriptive language appropriately.

- Setting

SEQUENCE

WARM UP

1. Ask: *Does anyone have examples for the Fiction Fanatic board?* Allow one or two students to share their cards (Handout 1.4) with the class.
2. Tell students they are going to have their first full writing workshop. In Lesson 1.1, they started free writing in response to a prompt. During this lesson, they will finish their response and prepare it for sharing with the class in their first writers' retreat.
3. Distribute workshop folders (see p. 33) and Handout 2.1: Writing Workshop Guidelines. Review the guidelines. This handout should remain in students' workshop folders.

Allow a few students to share Fiction Fanatic Card at the start of each lesson. Encourage students to create a new Fiction Fanatic Card (Handout 1.4) whenever they find an example. Tell students not to worry if they have difficulty finding an example or their example doesn't quite fit the definition. Mistakes help us grow as learners.

During every writing workshop, encourage students to respond to the prompts by writing about topics that interest them or that they are passionate about.

ACTIVITY: WRITING WORKSHOP

4. Review the prompt students began writing about in Lesson 1.1: *Choose one of the five senses. In approximately 100 words, describe what you had for lunch today using the sense you have chosen.*
5. Ask students to continue writing as much as they want in response to the prompt, using what they wrote in the last lesson or a new version in their writer's notebooks. They will need to save enough time to transfer their final response to their workshop folder in the allotted time.

Give students 5–10 minutes to continue writing in their writer's notebooks before giving them a one-minute warning. Then, allow for 5–10 minutes of writing and/or transfer of writing to their workshop folders. The responses are designed to be short, so even if students did not have a lot in their writer's notebooks, they will be able to participate in the writers' retreat.

2E

If you have students who have difficulty with writing, you can either act as a scribe for them or give them access to a computer or tablet so that they can craft a response. You may also allow them to respond using other assistive devices recommended by special education resource teachers/specialists.

6. When students finish, encourage them to pay particular attention to imagery and symbols in their writing. Have them take some time to look over their work and consider any revisions they might want to make (e.g., use more imagery, use stronger words, incorporate the perspective from another sense, etc.).
7. Ask students to form circle(s), either as a full class or groups of 3–4 for the writers' retreat. Each student should read his or her prompt response aloud and allow time (about 2–3 minutes per response) for students to offer constructive feedback. The retreats should not dominate the lesson.

Ideally, students should be grouped according to their readiness during writers' retreats. This will help ensure that students are challenged and are given feedback at the same level. Designate a different discussion leader during each retreat to take notes on the feedback students in his or her group receive; collect these notes to help you adjust groups as needed.

- These are general guidelines for the amount of time to spend on each section of the writing workshop. Adjust times depending on the amount of class time you have and the abilities of your students.
- Skim students' writer's notebooks throughout the unit to check and see which students may be having difficulty and which students need more challenge.

INSTRUCTION: WHAT IS SETTING?

8. Tell students: *Now we're going to move on to our next area of focus: setting. How do we define setting again?* Ensure that students know that setting involves both time and place.
9. Say: *In fiction, we sometimes use time and places that are real and sometimes we use time and places that are made up. Even though we can use real times and places in fiction, we always make up what happens to the characters.* Add *setting* to the word wall.

APPLICATION: SETTING

10. Invite students to find a comfortable place for listening. Remind students to enjoy the way the passage sounds, but to listen for details about the setting, particularly any sensory imagery they notice.
11. Read aloud the excerpt from Chapter 1 of *A Tree Grows in Brooklyn* by Betty Smith.
12. Ask: *Where does Francie live? How does she feel about where she lives? What can we tell about her neighborhood from her description? What is the tree like?* (Serene is peaceful, so she is content with the neighborhood; the neighborhood is cramped and crowded; she uses positive descriptors [e.g., radiated, lush, serene]; the tree is out-of-place, resilient, protective.)

Ask students if they have difficulty with any words in the passage. Tricky words might include: *serene, somber, shafted* (in this context, it is descriptive of how the sun is broken up by the buildings), *lushly, tenement, refined, flourished.*

Students may not know what a *tenement* is, especially if they are not from a city. There are some great pictures that you can display to help students visualize Francie's place better available at http://www.brooklynvisualheritage.org/sitesearch/results/tenements.

Highlight the idea of resiliency, which is key to the setting. Explain how overcoming obstacles like the difficult background and inequality (shown in the description of the neighborhood) is seen through the tree. This makes it a symbol of resiliency.

Ask: *In what ways are we like the tree? What examples of resiliency do you have from your own life?*

Because some readings are excerpts, the passages will often fall short of "publishable" expectations. Explain how the authors are on the right track, but that they have to be clear and consistent in order for their work to be published.

Ask: *What is our setting? How does is it different from where Francie lives? How is it the same?*

Focus on the rubric: Display Appendix A1: Road to Publishing: Imagery and Setting. As a class, decide how the excerpt from *A Tree Grows in Brooklyn* fits into this rubric. The idea is to expose students to the rubric so they will understand it for their final stories later in the unit.

PREPARATION: FOR NEXT LESSON

With remaining class time, have students complete Fiction Fanatic Card (Handout 1.4) for *setting*. Or, encourage students to think of an example and bring it for the next lesson.

13. (Optional) Have students bring in pictures of their homes/community for the next lesson. If you do not have students bring in pictures, make sure you have enough available so that all students will have a picture to use for the workshop (brochures, magazines, etc.).

HANDOUT 2.1

WRITING WORKSHOP GUIDELINES

WRITING WORKSHOPS

1. Free write (write down whatever is on your mind!) in your writer's notebook until you feel like you can respond to the prompt.
2. Then, respond to the prompt in your writer's notebook until you feel happy with your response.
3. Write out your submission to the writers' retreat and store it in your workshop folder.
4. Close your workshop folder and place it in the top left-hand corner of your work area to show you are ready for the retreat.
5. If you finish early, you may . . .
   - Continue to free write in your writer's notebook.
   - Create Fiction Fanatics Cards.
   - Read a novel of your choice.

WRITERS' RETREATS

1. Wait your turn to share. Everyone will get a chance to read his or her work out loud.
2. When it is your turn, read your response out loud so that everyone in your group can hear you.
   - If you do not feel comfortable reading out loud, it is okay to ask your teacher or a friend to read it out loud for you.
   - If you are in small groups, do not read as loud so that you do not disrupt the other groups.
3. Offer constructive criticism to your peers. Make suggestions, *not* corrections. Avoid words such as *should*, *wrong*, and *bad*.
   - I think ______________________ would be even better if you considered ______________________.

HANDOUT 2.1, CONTINUED

- I would like to know more about ______________________________.
- One way to make ____________________ even stronger would be to ______________________________.

4. Point out areas of strength so the authors know what they are doing well.
   - I liked how you ______________________________.
5. If you do not get a chance to share, but you have something to say, write it down and ask your teacher to hand it to the author later.

LESSON 3 Setting, Continued

MATERIALS

- Student writer's notebooks
- Student workshop folders
- Video: "Mark Twain: Hannibal, MO" (available at http://www.pbs.org/video/2188475738)
- Handout 1.4: Fiction Fanatic Card
- Handout 3.1: Formative Assessment 1

- Writers create stories to document and make sense of thoughts/feelings/understandings about themselves and the world around them.
- Writers use senses, emotions, and images to evoke connections between the text and the reader.

OBJECTIVES

Students will:

- respond to a variety of prompts creatively and thoughtfully,
- offer constructive criticism both verbally and in writing, and
- write a fictional narrative focusing on a single topic.

- Setting
- Sensory details
- Character

SEQUENCE

WARM UP

1. Tell students: *Today we are going to be writing about our setting, which is (name of your city, town, etc.). Many great authors use where they lived as inspiration for their writing, like Mark Twain.*
2. Show students the video about Mark Twain.
3. Explain that writers often create stories to help them document thoughts, feelings, and understandings about themselves and the world around them. Twain wanted to document what it felt like to be a child, so he wrote about where he grew up. Students will do the same in this lesson's writing workshop.

ACTIVITY: WRITING WORKSHOP

4. Set up three stations—people, place, and things. Distribute prompts at each station:
    - ✓ **People:** Based on the picture you have chosen, write 100 words about the people you see. If there are no people, think about the person who may have taken the photo. Choose one sensory detail (sight, hearing, taste, touch, smell) to focus on. If there is time left at the station, you may choose another sensory detail to write about.
    - ✓ **Place:** Based on the picture you have chosen, write 100 words about the place you see. Choose one sensory detail (sight, hearing, taste, touch, smell) to focus on. If there is time left at the station, you may choose another sensory detail to write about.
    - ✓ **Things:** Based on the picture you have chosen, write 100 words about the things you see. Choose one sensory detail (sight, hearing, taste, touch, smell) to focus on. If there is time left at the station, you may choose another sensory detail to write about.

5. Tell students: *Because we are just starting out, you are going to write small paragraphs about 100 words long, focusing on sensory details. To help you focus, you are going to use a picture of your community for inspiration. You can see we have three stations set up. At each station, you will write in your writer's notebook about either the people who are in the photo/who took the photo, the place where the picture was taken, or the things you see in the picture.*
6. Have students spend 5–10 minutes at each station.

After Writing Workshop 1, you may have an idea of which students find the writing process easier. Students who struggled with imagery and sensory details should start with Station 2 (place), move to Station 3 (things), and then end with Station 1 (people). Students who did well with imagery and sensory details should start with Station 1, move to Station 2, and end with Station 3. Students who scored in between should start with Station 3, move to Station 1, and end with Station 2.

7. When students have cycled through each station, ask them to choose which response they would like to transfer to their workshop folder. Explain that they should choose either the response they are happiest with, or the response that they think needs the most work.
8. Remind students of the guidelines for writers' retreats (Handout 2.1). Then, as a class or in their groups, have each student read his or her chosen prompt response aloud, and allow time (about 2–3 minutes per response) for students to offer constructive feedback. The retreats should not dominate the lesson.

PREPARATION: FORMATIVE ASSESSMENT 1

9. Say: *The responses we wrote about pictures today helped us understand our place, but it also introduced us to people and things. What literary term helps us better understand people and things?*
10. If necessary, lead students to the term *character* with questions: *What do we call the people in stories?* Provide a definition: A character is a person, animal, or any other thing with a personality that appears in a story. Ask students if they know of any works of fiction that have animals or things as characters to ensure they understand the definition. Add *character* to the word wall.
11. Tell students: *We are going to learn about different types of characters, but I want to see what you think they are first.* Distribute Handout 3.1: Formative Assessment. Students will circle the terms that they know describe characters, underline the terms that they think describe characters, and cross out the terms that do not describe characters.

With remaining class time, have students complete Fiction Fanatic Card (Handout 1.4) for *character*. Or, encourage students to think of an example and bring it for the next lesson.

HANDOUT 3.1

FORMATIVE ASSESSMENT 1

Directions: *Circle* the terms that you know describe characters. *Underline* the terms that you think describe characters. *Cross out* the terms that do not describe characters. Then, write the definitions of any terms that you know.

Abstract	Round
Antagonist	Sensory
Concrete	Static
Dynamic	Stock
Empathy	Stereotype
Flat	Sympathy
Protagonist	

LESSON 4 Characters

MATERIALS

- Student writer's notebooks
- Student workshop folders
- Teacher's copy of excerpt from *Peter Pan* by J. M. Barrie (available at http://www.gutenberg.org/files/16/16-h/16-h.htm)
- Student copies of Chapter 2 (pp. 11–13 , para. 1–17) from *Matilda* by Roald Dahl (Puffin, 2013)
- Student copies of Chapter 2 (pp. 12, 14–15, para. 1–2, 5–20) from *The Witches* by Roald Dahl (Puffin, 2013)
- Chart paper
- Handout 1.4: Fiction Fanatic Card
- Handout 4.1: Protagonist and Antagonist
- Handout 4.2: Round and Flat Characters
- Appendix A2: Road to Publishing: Characters

Literature is based on universal themes/characters/situations that embody the human experience and help us make sense of our own lives.

OBJECTIVES

Students will:

- read and demonstrate comprehension of fictional texts, and
- draw conclusions/make inferences about text.

- Stock character
- Stereotype
- Protagonist
- Antagonist

SEQUENCE

WARM UP

> Note which students do well and which students have more difficulty with the material in this lesson so you can use this information and Formative Assessment 1 to group students later.

1. Ask students to recall the definition of character. Remind students: *Characters are an important part of fiction. We connect with the characters in the stories we read when we find things about them that are familiar. One of the ways that authors can help readers connect with the story quickly is through the use of stock characters.*
2. Ask: *Can anyone guess what a stock character is?*
3. If necessary, guide students to the definition. Ask them if they know how to use the word *stock*, such as stocking shelves. Just as there are multiple boxes of Lucky Charms on grocery store shelves, there are multiple characters that fit under a certain label. Stock characters are types of characters that are regularly used in fiction. Add *stock character* to the word wall.
4. Explain that stock characters are very similar to stereotypes. Stock characters appear over and over in different stories—they are a formulaic type. Because these character types are very predictable, they might also be called stereotypes because they are so familiar and simple. Stock characters often appear along with motifs, which also repeat.
5. (Optional) If students struggled with *stereotype* and *motif* on the unit preassessment, remind students that a *stereotype* is a character that is simple, usually described with one or two words. For example, stories often reinforce the stereotype of a beautiful princess. A *motif* is an important event or thing that occurs over and over in stories. Fairy tales often use motifs, such as a peasant girl becoming a princess. Add these terms to the word wall.

APPLICATION: STOCK CHARACTER

6. Ask: *Think about Alice in* Alice's Adventures in Wonderland. *Does she sound like a stock character?* Let students respond and guide them to the answer: Alice is not a stock character. A stock or stereotypical character would be instantly recognizable, like how Sven, the reindeer in *Frozen*, is a sidekick.
7. Have students think for a few minutes about types of stock characters they often see in literature, writing down their thoughts on scratch paper. Then, have them work in pairs to compare lists.
8. Afterward, have students share their responses and brainstorm a list of types of stock characters students might see as you read. Display the list. Aim for 5–10 types of stock characters (e.g., princess, prince, villain, hero, sidekick, etc.).

> If you need a reference, check out the list of stock characters available at http://www.worldlibrary.org/articles/list_of_stock_characters. Your list does not need to be as extensive.

9. Invite students to find a comfortable place for listening. Ask students to take notes in their writer's notebooks about details that make them think a character fits a certain type.
10. Read aloud an excerpt from Chapter 4 of *Peter Pan* by J. M. Barrie ("Sometimes he poised himself in the air . . ." through "'I promise,' John said loyally.")
11. Ask: *What stock characters do we see here?* Students should note hero (Peter) and villain (Hook); they may also choose sidekick (John) or mother figure (Wendy). Identifying hero and villain is the most important.

In the sections students will read in this lesson, there are many power dynamics. In *Peter Pan*, Peter is the leader of the group, and they all defer to him. In *Matilda*, Matilda's father makes it clear she does not need to read and she defies him. In *The Witches*, the narrator looks up to his grandmother and she listens to him. Discuss what a healthy dynamic looks like in different situations, like at school and at home.

ACTIVITY: GROUP CHARACTER STUDY

12. Tell students: *You are doing a great job of talking about different types of characters, but there are other terms that we can use to distinguish different characters from one another.*

Assign students to groups of 4–5 based on Formative Assessment 1. The lower scoring groups will work on Handout 4.1: Protagonist and Antagonist and read an excerpt from *The Witches* by Roald Dahl. The higher scoring groups will work Handout 4.2: Round and Flat Characters and read an excerpt from *Matilda* by Roald Dahl. You may also choose to use excerpts from other works with clearly identifiable protagonists/antagonists and round/flat details from your classroom library.

13. Tell students: *Your job is to read the passage, then identify the characters you think might fit the terms together as a group. It is okay to guess, but make sure you can tell me why you think the characters might fit that term.* Once groups have identified the correct characters, distribute chart paper. *You will work together with your group to develop definitions for the terms based on what you have read.*
14. As students work, make sure they understand that protagonists are not always good, and antagonists are not always bad. Have students come up with examples of "bad" protagonists and "good" antagonists (e.g., the Grinch and the Whos). For the round/flat group, have them think about what images come to mind when they think of round and flat objects, and help them make the connection between these ideas and how these images can apply to characters.

15. Afterward, have each group present their terms and examples to the rest of the class. Ask the protagonist and antagonist groups if they can tell which characters are round and flat and vice versa. Make sure that students understand that there are always identifiable protagonists and antagonists in short stories, but they may not be able to note round or flat characters as much because of the shorter length. When they write their stories, they will definitely have protagonists/antagonists, but whether they have round or flat characters will depend on how they write their stories.
16. Add *protagonist* and *antagonist* to the word wall.

Focus on the rubric: Display Appendix A2: Road to Publishing: Characters. As a class, decide how the excerpt from *Peter Pan* fits into this rubric. The idea is to expose students to the rubric so they will understand it for their final stories later in the unit.

PREPARATION: FOR NEXT LESSON

If time permits, allow students to complete Fiction Fanatic Card (Handout 1.4) for *stock characters*, *protagonist*, *antagonist*, *round character*, and *flat character*.

HANDOUT 4.1

PROTAGONIST AND ANTAGONIST

Directions: Read your assigned passage. Then, with your group, develop definitions for the terms below.

Protagonist
Definition:

Antagonist
Definition:

HANDOUT 4.2

ROUND AND FLAT CHARACTERS

Directions: Read your assigned passage. Then, with your group, develop definitions for the terms below.

Round Characters
Definition:

Flat Characters
Definition:

LESSON 5

Characterization

MATERIALS

- ✓ Student writer's notebooks
- ✓ Student workshop folders
- ✓ Teacher's copy of Chapter 1 (pp. 5–9, para. 1–8) of *From the Mixed-Up Files of Mrs. Basil E. Frankweiler* by E. L. Konigsburg (Atheneum, 2013; also available at http://www.washingtonpost.com/wp-dyn/articles/A61069-2004Jun22.html)
- ✓ Teacher's copy of Chapter 2 (pp. 11–13, para. 1–17) from *Matilda* by Roald Dahl (Puffin, 2013; also available at http://www.npr.org/books/titles/205190773/matilda#excerpt)
- ✓ Handout 1.4: Fiction Fanatic Card
- ✓ Appendix B3: Road to Publishing: Characterization

- Literature is based on universal themes/characters/situations that embody the human experience and help us make sense of our own lives.
- Writers use senses, emotions, and images to evoke connections between the text and the reader.

OBJECTIVES

Students will:

- ✓ use brainstorming to generate ideas at the prewriting stage of composition,
- ✓ identify and use different story devices to enrich narrative writing, and
- ✓ identify different characteristics in a fictional narrative.

- Major character
- Minor character
- Direct characterization
- Indirect characterization

SEQUENCE

WARM UP

1. Tell students: *There are a few types of characters that we did not discuss in the last lesson. Like protagonist and antagonist, and round and flat characters, they are easy to discuss in pairs. The pair we are going to talk about briefly today are major and minor characters.*
2. Ask students: *Who thinks they can define these terms?* Students should understand that major characters are important to the development of the story, while minor characters are only a part of the story momentarily. Even though they are not in the entire story, minor characters can contribute by providing important information about the major characters, or by adding lighter moments to break the tension.
3. Read the excerpt from *Matilda* by Roald Dahl. Have students discuss who would be an example of a minor character in this passage (the librarian). Ask: *What makes this character a minor character?* (The character does not really change the story in any way.) Add *major character* and *minor character* to the word wall.

At the start of each lesson, check in with students to see if they brought in any Fiction Fanatic Card (Handout 1.4) about characters, or any of the other topics discussed thus far.

If students are still having trouble distinguishing between major and minor characters, brainstorm a list of minor and major characters in stories with students that they might be familiar with. For example, minor characters include Skunk in *Bambi*, Duke of Weselton in *Frozen*, or Templeton in *Charlotte's Web*. Record student responses on the board.

4. Tell students they may have noticed that a lot of the major characters they've discussed are protagonists. They are also round. Say: *That is because it is more interesting to read a story focused on a character that we know a lot about. That way, we can see them change and develop. Think about a growth mindset. As people, we can always be learning and changing, and we like to see that in fiction as well. Keep that in mind as we complete today's writing workshop. The workshops should be about engaging in the process of writing, and the retreats should be a time for you to get feedback so you can grow as a writer.*

Growth mindset (Dweck, 2006) is when students believe they can grow their intelligence and achievement through effort and hard work. The opposite is a *fixed mindset*, when students believe there is nothing they can do to become more intelligent, so they do not put in effort when they do not understand something. Throughout the unit, remind your students that you believe they can become better writers with effort and practice. Acknowledge when you see them improve, especially through hard work.

ACTIVITY: WRITING WORKSHOP

5. Introduce the following prompts:
   - ✓ Using only sensory details, write 100 words to describe a person so that a bad feeling toward the person is evident to the reader.
   - ✓ Using only sensory details, write 100 words to describe a person so that a good feeling toward the person is evident to the reader.

6. Ask students to choose one of the prompts to respond to in their Writer's Notebooks. They can write as much as they want in response to the prompt during the time allotted for the workshop in their writer's notebooks. However, they will need to make sure to save enough time to transfer their final responses to their workshop folders.
7. Give students 5–10 minutes before giving them a one-minute warning. Then, allow for 5–10 minutes (maximum) of writing and/or transfer of writing. The responses are designed to be short, so even if students did not have a lot in their writer's notebooks, they will be able to participate in the writers' retreat.

2E

Remember:

- During every writing workshop, encourage students to respond to the prompts by writing about topics that interest them or that they are passionate about.
- If you have students who have difficulty with writing, you can either act as a scribe for them, or give them access to a computer/tablet so that they can craft a response. You may also allow them to respond using other assistive devices recommended by special education resource teachers/specialists.

8. Ask students to form circle(s) either as a full class or groups of 3–4 for the writers' retreat. Each student should read his or her prompt response aloud and allow time (about 2–3 minutes per response) for students to offer constructive feedback. The retreat should not dominate the lesson.

Ideally, students should be grouped according to their readiness during writers' retreats. This will help ensure that students are challenged and are given feedback at the same level. Designate a different discussion leader during each retreat to take notes on the feedback students in his or her group receive; collect these notes to help you adjust groups as needed.

This activity will work best if students are sitting in a circle, so they are all part of the group rather than having to stand in front of their peers. If students are shy and do not want to share, they can ask a classmate or the teacher to read the response aloud for the—the goal is for students to get feedback. As the unit progresses, continue to encourage the children to read their own work out loud.

9. Encourage students to pay particular attention to the sensory details each author used to illuminate the good or bad feeling toward the character. Try to model constructive criticism by highlighting one common aspect of the writers' retreat to reinforce (e.g., a couple of great examples of creating a feeling toward a character using sensory details).

INSTRUCTION: WHAT IS CHARACTERIZATION?

10. Tell students they are going to learn about characterization. Ask: *Do you remember what the* -tion *suffix means?*
11. Tell students that *-tion* indicates an act or process. That means that characterization is the act or process of creating a character. When they used sensory details to describe a good or bad character, they were

characterizing them as good or bad. This is considered *indirect characterization* because students were using the details to show if the character was good or bad. *Direct characterization* is where the reader is told what the character is like.

12. Add *direct characterization* and *indirect characterization* to the word wall.
13. Tell students: *Let's read an example that has both types of characterization to see if we can tell the difference.* Invite students to find a comfortable place for listening. Remind them that they will want to listen for both direct and indirect characterization.
14. Read aloud an excerpt from *From the Mixed-Up Files of Mrs. Basil E. Frankweiler* by E. L. Konigsburg. Konigsburg was born in New York City but grew up a small town in Pennsylvania. She was inspired to write *From the Mixed-Up Files* by her children, as she felt that if they ever ran away they would never consider anything less elegant than the Metropolitan Museum of Art.

"The Mixed-Up Kids of Mrs. E. L. Konigsburg" by Marah Guber (available at http://www.publicbooks.org/fiction/the-mixed-up-kids-of-mrs-e-l-konigsburg) has great, introspective information about the author's works. In particular, Guber notes an important component of growth mindset shown by Claudia—that the act of preparing for something is often more important than the result. What Claudia learns about herself when she runs away is more important than the fact that she runs away.

15. Ask: *What examples of direct characterization do you see? What examples of indirect characterization do you see?* Write student responses on the board, correcting them as needed. Make sure students feel confident with the topics before moving in to more critical discussions.

Ask: *Why do authors use both direct and indirect characterization?* Help students understand that readers do not need all the details spelled out for them. Plus, writing that spells everything out would be very boring to read. Indirect characterization allows readers to think and write more creatively.

You might also note that Claudia is running away because she feels an injustice has been done to her. Ask: *Based on what is presented about Claudia, do you agree with this injustice? Why or why not?*

Focus on the rubric: Display Appendix A3: Road to Publishing: Characterization. As a class, decide how the excerpt from *From the Mixed-Up Files of Mrs. Basil E. Frankweiler* fits into this rubric. The idea is to expose students to the rubric so they will understand it for their final stories later in the unit.

With any time remaining, students can complete Fiction Fanatic cards (Handout 1.4) on *direct characterization* and *indirect characterization*. Or, encourage students to think of an example and bring it to the next lesson.

LESSON 6 Dialogue

MATERIALS

- ✓ Student writer's notebooks
- ✓ Handout 1.4: Fiction Fanatic Card
- ✓ Handout 6.1A: *Peter Pan*—No Dialogue
- ✓ Handout 6.1B: *Peter Pan*—Dialogue Only
- ✓ Handout 6.1C: *Peter Pan*—Full Version
- ✓ Handout 6.2A: *Peter Pan* Activity—No Dialogue
- ✓ Handout 6.2B: *Peter Pan* Activity—Dialogue Only
- ✓ Handout 6.2C. *Peter Pan* Activity—Full Version
- ✓ Handout 6.3: Formative Assessment 2
- ✓ Appendix A4: Road to Publishing: Dialogue

- Writers use senses, emotions, and images to evoke connections between the text and the reader.
- Different perspectives and opinions of an event are legitimate when justified by evidence.

OBJECTIVES

Students will:

- ✓ identify the elements of story structure in a fictional narrative,
- ✓ identify the structure of a fictional narrative using specific examples from the text,
- ✓ identify and use different types of sentences to enhance a narrative/ story, and
- ✓ engage the reader with sentence and word variety.

- Dialogue

SEQUENCE

WARM UP

1. Tell students that during the last lesson they learned about direct and indirect characterization. Ask:
   - ✓ *Who can give me an example of direct characterization?* Students should give you an example that states a fact about a character.
   - ✓ *If I walked over to the desk and slammed my hand down on the desk, what would you think?* Students should say that you are mad or angry.
   - ✓ *Would this be an example of direct or indirect characterization?* Indirect.
   - ✓ Right! So we show how we feel with our actions just as much as we do with our words. That is why we use both direct and indirect characterization. We also learn a lot about characters from what they say. Do you know what it's called when characters have a conversation?

2. Once students recognize that *dialogue* is a conversation between two or more people, ask: *How do authors use dialogue?* Discuss this, pointing out that that authors are showing interaction between characters.
3. Ask: *Why do authors use dialogue?* Discuss that authors are showing how characters interact, and that they are also showing different characters' perspectives by allowing them to state their thoughts and feelings. Dialogue helps readers to see the reasons why characters act in certain ways. Add *dialogue* to the word wall.

INSTRUCTION: DIALOGUE

4. Tell students that they are going to take a closer look at dialogue by investigating how their perception of an event changes when they see something with and without dialogue.
5. Display and/or distribute Handout 6.1A: *Peter Pan*—No Dialogue. Ask: *What can we tell about what is happening here?* Students should note the following:
   - ✓ Peter, Wendy, John, and Michael are all present for the conversation;
   - ✓ John and Michael seem scared/afraid ("crying," "speaking in gulps," "huskily"); and
   - ✓ Peter dislikes Hook ("hated word," then a reference to Hook).

   If they have other answers, make sure they can validate their responses with the text. Record students' response on the board.

6. Then, display and/or distribute Handout 6.1B: *Peter Pan*—Dialogue Only. Ask: *What does the dialogue tell us?* Students should note the following: (1) There is an adventure, (2) someone wants to kill a pirate, (3) they are afraid of Hook, who is the worst, (4) someone cut off Hook's right hand, and (5) someone pledges to let someone else take care of Hook. Explain to students that there is not enough in the dialogue itself to tell us who is speaking to whom.
7. Display and/or distribute Handout 6.3C: Peter Pan—Full Version. Ask: *If we combine the text and dialogue, do we get a clearer understanding of what is happening in the story? Why or why not?* Students should have a clearer understanding, because they need the text to understand who is speaking when. They also get a better sense of the way the characters feel. The dialogue helps to clarify what the relationship between Hook and Peter is like.

ACTIVITY: PUTTING IT TOGETHER

8. Have students work in pairs. Distribute Handouts 6.2A and 6.2B. One student in each pair should receive the passage without dialogue, while the other receives the passage with just dialogue.
9. Have students read their passages and compare summaries with their partners. Together, they should develop a final summary of the passage. When they finish, they should work together to make a list of punctuation and words that the author uses with dialogue. Provide students with 10–15 minutes to work on this.
10. Read the complete passage out loud (Handout 6.2C), and then allow 3–4 pairs to volunteer their summaries. Note any differences, and reinforce the idea that both components are necessary so that authors can make sure the reader understands the story.
11. Ask: *What about punctuation that goes along with dialogue? What do we need to add when we write?* Students should have (1) quotation marks, (2) end punctuation—periods/question marks/exclamation points, and (3) continuing punctuation—commas and em dashes. Point out the punctuation marks in the passage so all students can see them.
12. Make sure students understand that quotation marks go before and after the words that a character says, that commas and em dashes are used when the sentence is going to continue, and that periods end a sentence normally, question marks are used when a character is asking a question, and exclamation points are used when a character is speaking emphatically or louder. Point out any examples you see in the passage.
13. Tell students: *You will want to keep this punctuation in mind as you write your own dialogue. Now, let's try to list some of the words that the author used instead of "said." It would be pretty boring if we used "said"*

every time someone spoke. In the passages, point out ways in which the reader is made aware of dialogue (i.e., how readers know someone spoke or is speaking). There are four things to be aware of: (1) words instead of *said*, (2) adverbs, (3) action phrases, and (4) directives.

14. As a class, make a list of as many of the words in the four categories that you can find used in the selected passage. Consider doing this on chart paper or another display method if you want to save it and add more examples later.

Display Appendix B4: Road to Publishing: Dialogue. As a class, decide how the excerpts from *Peter Pan* fit into this rubric. The idea is to expose students to the rubric so they will understand it for their summative product later in the unit.

ACTIVITY: CONVERSATIONS

15. Ask students to have a short conversation with their partners about recess. They should write the conversation word for word in their writer's notebooks. They will use it in the next writing workshop. Provide students with one to two minutes for this conversation.

If possible, have students record their conversations and play them back to write them in their notebooks. This could be with a computer recording, tape recording, iPad, etc.

PREPARATION: FORMATIVE ASSESSMENT 2

16. Tell students: *Perspective is often conveyed through point of view, which we will discuss in the next class. To get a better understanding of your knowledge of point of view, I would like you to complete this short assessment.*
17. Distribute Handout 6.3: Formative Assessment 2 for students to complete.

With any time remaining, students can complete Fiction Fanatic cards (Handout 1.4) on *dialogue*. Or, encourage students to think of an example and bring it in for the next lesson.

HANDOUT 6.1A

PETER PAN—NO DIALOGUE

Directions: Read the following passage from J. M. Barrie's *Peter Pan*. It has been edited so there is no dialogue. What do you think is happening in this scene?

Sometimes he poised himself in the air, listening intently, with his hand to his ear, and again he would stare down with eyes so bright that they seemed to bore two holes to earth. Having done these things, he went on again.

His courage was almost appalling. He said casually to John.

Wendy said quickly, and Michael pressed her hand in gratitude, but the braver John hesitated.

He asked cautiously.

Peter told him.

John said after a long pause.

John said, a little huskily.

Peter spoke indignantly.

John decided to have tea first. He asked if there were many pirates on the island just now, and Peter said he had never known so many.

Answered Peter, and his face became very stern as he said that hated word.

Then indeed Michael began to cry, and even John could speak in gulps only, for they knew Hook's reputation.

John whispered huskily.

Said Peter sharply.

Peter continued.

John paled.

John said loyally.

HANDOUT 6.1B

PETER PAN—DIALOGUE ONLY

Directions: Read the following passage from J. M. Barrie's *Peter Pan*. It has been edited so there is only dialogue. What do you think is happening in this scene?

"Would you like an adventure now, or would you like to have your tea first?"

"What kind of adventure?"

"There's a pirate asleep in the pampas just beneath us. If you like, we'll go down and kill him."

"I don't see him."

"I do."

"Suppose he were to wake up."

"You don't think I would kill him while he was sleeping! I would wake him first, and then kill him. That's the way I always do."

"I say! Do you kill many?"

"Tons."

"How ripping."

"Who is captain now?"

"Hook." "Jas. Hook?"

"Ay."

"He was Blackbeard's bo'sun. He is the worst of them all. He is the only man of whom Barbecue was afraid."

"That's him,"

"What is he like? Is he big?"

"He is not so big as he was."

"How do you mean?"

"I cut off a bit of him."

HANDOUT 6.1B, CONTINUED

"You!"

"Yes, me."

"I wasn't meaning to be disrespectful."

"Oh, all right."

"But, I say, what bit?" "His right hand."

"Then he can't fight now?"

"Oh, can't he just!"

"Left-hander?"

"He has an iron hook instead of a right hand, and he claws with it."

"Claws!"

"I say, John,"

"Yes."

"Say, 'Ay, ay, sir.'"

"Ay, ay, sir."

"There is one thing that every boy who serves under me has to promise, and so must you. It is this, if we meet Hook in open fight, you must leave him to me."

"I promise."

HANDOUT 6.1C

PETER PAN—FULL VERSION

Directions: Read the following passage from J. M. Barrie's *Peter Pan*. It has both text and dialogue. Do you get a clearer understanding of what is happening in this scene?

Sometimes he poised himself in the air, listening intently, with his hand to his ear, and again he would stare down with eyes so bright that they seemed to bore two holes to earth. Having done these things, he went on again.

His courage was almost appalling. "Would you like an adventure now," he said casually to John, "or would you like to have your tea first?"

Wendy said "tea first" quickly, and Michael pressed her hand in gratitude, but the braver John hesitated.

"What kind of adventure?" he asked cautiously.

"There's a pirate asleep in the pampas just beneath us," Peter told him. "If you like, we'll go down and kill him."

"I don't see him," John said after a long pause.

"I do."

"Suppose," John said, a little huskily, "he were to wake up."

Peter spoke indignantly. "You don't think I would kill him while he was sleeping! I would wake him first, and then kill him. That's the way I always do."

"I say! Do you kill many?"

"Tons."

John said "How ripping," but decided to have tea first. He asked if there were many pirates on the island just now, and Peter said he had never known so many.

"Who is captain now?"

"Hook," answered Peter, and his face became very stern as he said that hated word.

"Jas. Hook?"

HANDOUT 6.1C, CONTINUED

"Ay."

Then indeed Michael began to cry, and even John could speak in gulps only, for they knew Hook's reputation.

"He was Blackbeard's bo'sun," John whispered huskily. "He is the worst of them all. He is the only man of whom Barbecue was afraid."

"That's him," said Peter.

"What is he like? Is he big?"

"He is not so big as he was."

"How do you mean?"

"I cut off a bit of him."

"You!"

"Yes, me," said Peter sharply.

"I wasn't meaning to be disrespectful."

"Oh, all right."

"But, I say, what bit?"

"His right hand."

"Then he can't fight now?"

"Oh, can't he just!"

"Left-hander?"

"He has an iron hook instead of a right hand, and he claws with it."

"Claws!"

"I say, John," said Peter.

"Yes."

"Say, 'Ay, ay, sir.'"

"Ay, ay, sir."

"There is one thing," Peter continued, "that every boy who serves under me has to promise, and so must you."

John paled.

"It is this, if we meet Hook in open fight, you must leave him to me."

"I promise," John said loyally.

HANDOUT 6.2A

PETER PAN ACTIVITY—NO DIALOGUE

Directions: Read the following passage from J. M. Barrie's *Peter Pan*. It has been edited so there is no dialogue. Compare the summary of your passage with your partner's, the passage with only dialogue. Then, work together to develop a final summary of the passage.

Peter, seeing this to be a good idea, at once pretended that it was his own. The house was quite beautiful, and no doubt Wendy was very cosy within, though, of course, they could no longer see her. Peter strode up and down, ordering finishing touches. Nothing escaped his eagle eyes. Just when it seemed absolutely finished:

He said.

They were very ashamed, but Tootles gave the sole of his shoe, and it made an excellent knocker.

Absolutely finished now, they thought.

Not a bit of it. Peter said.

Said John importantly. This gave Peter an idea. He snatched the hat off John's head, knocked out the bottom [top], and put the hat on the roof. The little house was so pleased to have such a capital chimney that, as if to say thank you, smoke immediately began to come out of the hat.

Now really and truly it was finished. Nothing remained to do but to knock.

Peter warned them.

He was glad no one asked him what first impressions are; they were all too busy looking their best.

He knocked politely, and now the wood was as still as the children, not a sound to be heard except from Tinker Bell, who was watching from a branch and openly sneering.

What the boys were wondering was, would any one answer the knock? If a lady, what would she be like?

HANDOUT 6.2A, CONTINUED

The door opened and a lady came out. It was Wendy. They all whipped off their hats.

She looked properly surprised, and this was just how they had hoped she would look.

She said.

Of course Slightly was the first to get his word in. He said rapidly.

Cried Nibs.

Wendy said, and they were the very words they had hoped she would say.

Cried the twins.

Then all went on their knees, and holding out their arms cried.

Wendy said, all shining.

Said Peter, as if he were the only person present who knew all about it, though he was really the one who knew least.

Wendy said.

They all cried.

She said.

In they went; I don't know how there was room for them, but you can squeeze very tight in the Neverland. And that was the first of the many joyous evenings they had with Wendy. By and by she tucked them up in the great bed in the home under the trees, but she herself slept that night in the little house, and Peter kept watch outside with drawn sword, for the pirates could be heard carousing far away and the wolves were on the prowl. The little house looked so cozy and safe in the darkness, with a bright light showing through its blinds, and the chimney smoking beautifully, and Peter standing on guard. After a time he fell asleep, and some unsteady fairies had to climb over him on their way home. Any of the other boys obstructing the fairy path at night they would have mischiefed, but they just tweaked Peter's nose and passed on.

HANDOUT 6.2B

PETER PAN ACTIVITY—DIALOGUE ONLY

Directions: Read the following passage from J. M. Barrie's *Peter Pan*. It has been edited so there is only dialogue. Compare the summary of your passage with your partner's, the passage without dialogue. Then, work together to develop a final summary of the passage.

"There's no knocker on the door."

"There's no chimney, we must have a chimney."

"It certainly does need a chimney."

"All look your best; first impressions are awfully important."

"Where am I?"

"Wendy lady, for you we built this house."

"Oh, say you're pleased."

"Lovely, darling house."

"And we are your children."

"O Wendy lady, be our mother."

"Ought I? Of course it's frightfully fascinating, but you see I am only a little girl. I have no real experience."

"That doesn't matter. What we need is just a nice motherly person."

"Oh dear! You see, I feel that is exactly what I am."

"It is, it is; we saw it at once."

"Very well, I will do my best. Come inside at once, you naughty children; I am sure your feet are damp. And before I put you to bed I have just time to finish the story of Cinderella."

HANDOUT 6.2C

PETER PAN ACTIVITY—FULL VERSION

Directions: Read the following passage from J. M. Barrie's *Peter Pan*. It has both text and dialogue. Do you get a clearer understanding of what is happening in this scene?

Peter, seeing this to be a good idea, at once pretended that it was his own. The house was quite beautiful, and no doubt Wendy was very cosy within, though, of course, they could no longer see her. Peter strode up and down, ordering finishing touches. Nothing escaped his eagle eyes. Just when it seemed absolutely finished:

"There's no knocker on the door," he said.

They were very ashamed, but Tootles gave the sole of his shoe, and it made an excellent knocker.

Absolutely finished now, they thought.

Not a bit of it. "There's no chimney," Peter said; "we must have a chimney."

"It certainly does need a chimney," said John importantly. This gave Peter an idea. He snatched the hat off John's head, knocked out the bottom [top], and put the hat on the roof. The little house was so pleased to have such a capital chimney that, as if to say thank you, smoke immediately began to come out of the hat.

Now really and truly it was finished. Nothing remained to do but to knock.

"All look your best," Peter warned them; "first impressions are awfully important."

He was glad no one asked him what first impressions are; they were all too busy looking their best.

He knocked politely, and now the wood was as still as the children, not a sound to be heard except from Tinker Bell, who was watching from a branch and openly sneering.

HANDOUT 6.2C, CONTINUED

What the boys were wondering was, would any one answer the knock? If a lady, what would she be like?

The door opened and a lady came out. It was Wendy. They all whipped off their hats.

She looked properly surprised, and this was just how they had hoped she would look.

"Where am I?" she said.

Of course Slightly was the first to get his word in. "Wendy lady," he said rapidly, "for you we built this house."

"Oh, say you're pleased," cried Nibs.

"Lovely, darling house," Wendy said, and they were the very words they had hoped she would say.

"And we are your children," cried the twins.

Then all went on their knees, and holding out their arms cried, "O Wendy lady, be our mother."

"Ought I?" Wendy said, all shining. "Of course it's frightfully fascinating, but you see I am only a little girl. I have no real experience."

"That doesn't matter," said Peter, as if he were the only person present who knew all about it, though he was really the one who knew least. "What we need is just a nice motherly person."

"Oh dear!" Wendy said, "you see, I feel that is exactly what I am."

"It is, it is," they all cried; "we saw it at once."

"Very well," she said, "I will do my best. Come inside at once, you naughty children; I am sure your feet are damp. And before I put you to bed I have just time to finish the story of Cinderella."

In they went; I don't know how there was room for them, but you can squeeze very tight in the Neverland. And that was the first of the many joyous evenings they had with Wendy. By and by she tucked them up in the great bed in the home under the trees, but she herself slept that night in the little house, and Peter kept watch outside with drawn sword, for the

HANDOUT 6.2C, CONTINUED

pirates could be heard carousing far away and the wolves were on the prowl. The little house looked so cozy and safe in the darkness, with a bright light showing through its blinds, and the chimney smoking beautifully, and Peter standing on guard. After a time he fell asleep, and some unsteady fairies had to climb over him on their way home. Any of the other boys obstructing the fairy path at night they would have mischiefed, but they just tweaked Peter's nose and passed on.

HANDOUT 6.3

FORMATIVE ASSESSMENT 2

Directions: Next to each sentence, write:

- **1** if you think it is a first person narrator.
- **2** if you think it is a second person narrator.
- **3** if you think it is a third person narrator.

1. ______ When I told them my story, they were shocked.
2. ______ You're afraid of what you'll find when you open the door, but you still turn the handle.
3. ______ He did not think that the punishment was fair.
4. ______ Our view of the game was spectacular.
5. ______ They were surprised by the clanging sounds coming from the attic.
6. ______ My feelings are hurt, but I don't want anyone to know, so I smile.
7. ______ You walked to the end of the road before you turned around.
8. ______ His aunt was waiting for him in the car.
9. ______ We all stayed in the basement until the storm was over.
10. ______ She is waiting for her friend to come back from vacation.

LESSON

7 Point of View

MATERIALS

- Student writer's notebooks
- Student workshop folders
- Student copies of Chapter 1 (pp. 1–3, para. 1–4) from *Return to the Cave of Time* by Edward Packard (Simon & Schuster, 2010)
- Student copies of Chapter 1 (pp. 5–7, para. 1–12) from *Cool Zone With the Pain and the Great One* by Judy Blume (Random House, 2008)
- Student copies of Chapter 1 (p. 3, para. 1–5) from *Wonder* by R. J. Palacio (Knopf, 2012)
- Image: "Girl With Cat" (available at http://thegraphicsfairy.com/public-domain-download-girl-cat-sweet)
- Handout 1.4: Fiction Fanatic Card
- Handout 7.1: First- and Second-Person Point of View
- Handout 7.2: What's Best for My Story?

- Literature is based on universal themes/characters/situations that embody the human experience and help us make sense of our own lives.
- Writers create stories to document and make sense of thoughts/feelings/understandings about themselves and the world around them.
- Different perspectives and opinions of an event are legitimate when justified by evidence.

OBJECTIVES

Students will:

- identify the narrator and point of view from which a fictional narrative is told,
- respond to a variety of prompts creatively and thoughtfully, and
- offer constructive criticism both verbally and in writing.

- First-person point of view
- Second-person point of view

SEQUENCE

ACTIVITY: WRITING WORKSHOP

1. Introduce the following prompt: *In a one-page response, fictionalize the conversation you wrote down in the last lesson. Use both dialogue and actions to show characterization.*
2. Ask students to respond to the prompt in their writer's notebooks. Give students 5–10 minutes before giving them a one-minute warning. Then, allow for 5–10 minutes of writing and/or transfer of writing to their workshop folders.
3. Ask students to form circle(s) (either as a full class or groups of 3–4) for the writers' retreat. Each student should read his or her prompt response aloud and allow time (about 2–3 minutes per response) for students to offer constructive feedback.
4. Encourage students to pay particular attention to whether the characterization is direct or indirect, and how students use dialogue. Try to model constructive criticism by highlighting one common aspect of the writers' retreat to reinforce (e.g., see if you can add to the list of words that can replace "said").

INSTRUCTION: WHO TELLS THE STORY?

5. Say: *During the writing workshop, you wrote about characters during recess. I want to think about the narrator.* Select one student's prompt response from the writers' retreat. Ask: *Who do you think is telling the story?* Write students' responses on the board, and ask them what pronouns they used for their narrator.
6. Tell students that narration is how the story is told. Narration is usually talked about through point of view, which is the perspective through which the story is told. There are three different kinds of point of view: first, second, and third person. In this lesson, students will work in groups to understand first and second person. Each group will answer the following questions:
   - ✓ Which pronouns does the narrator in first person/second person use?
   - ✓ How do the pronouns make us feel about what we are reading?
7. Assign students to groups based on the results of Formative Assessment 2.

- **Group A** (1–4 questions correct on the formative assessment) will read from *Return to the Cave of Time* by Edward Packard.
- **Group B** (5–7 questions correct) will read from *Cool Zone With the Pain and the Great One* by Judy Blume.
- **Group C** (8–10 questions correct) will read from *Wonder* by R. J. Palacio (ending with "Whatever you're thinking, it's probably worse.")

If students had similar answers to Formative Assessment 2 and you do not have four groups, you may consider matching students in groups with similar reading levels. Group A is simplest passage.

8. Have each group record its responses on the board.
9. Distribute Handout 7.1 First- and Second-Person Point of View. Review groups' answers and generate classroom definitions, making it clear that *second person* has the narrator address the reader as a character and *first person* has major characters narrating the story.
10. Introduce first-person plural as needed. Students should note the difference in pronouns between first-person singular and plural (I vs. we). When writers use the pronouns *we*, *us*, or *our*, it is first-person plural because there are multiple narrators.
11. Students should also note that sometimes the narrators are talking about themselves, and sometimes they are talking about someone else. When they are talking about themselves, they are the main character. When they are talking about someone else, they are an observer.

The first-person narrators in *Cool Zone With the Pain and the Great One* and *Wonder* can help students understand how the world can feel unfair. In the former, the narrator is jealous of her little brother, though the author will go back and forth between their point of view in the novel so that the reader can understand where each character's feelings come from. The passage from *Wonder*, in which the main character has a disability, helps students understand how someone with different capabilities works through that situation.

12. Add *first-person point of view* and *second-person point of view* to the word wall.

ACTIVITY: POINT OF VIEW

13. Tell students: *We are going to make sure we understand the differences between first and second person. To do this, we are going to write sentences about a picture.*
14. Display the "Girl With Cat" image. Say: *The girl is going to be our narrator, so you are going to want to think about what is happening from her perspective. What would a first-person narrator say about what is happening?*
15. Choose 2–3 students to share, writing their responses on the board. See if you get a variety of responses (singular, plural, main, observer). If not,

Distribute Handout 7.2: What's Best For My Story? to help students start thinking about the perspective they would like to use to tell their own story. The handout also includes third-person point of view, which will be explored in Lesson 8. Review the handout as a class, or have students keep it in their workshop folders as a guide.

prompt students to provide the other responses (e.g., *What would the sentence be if both the girl and the cat were narrators? What would the sentence be if the girl was an observer?*). Sentences may include:

- **Singular, main:** I am holding the cat's bowl.
- **Singular, observer:** The cat sits quietly as I hold the bowl.
- **Plural, main:** We are outside in the garden.

16. Ask: *What would a second-person narrator say about what is happening?* (You are waiting for me to give the cat its water bowl.)
17. If students say a sentence like "You are waiting for me to give you water," explain that it is still second person. It just means that the reader is in the role of the cat. Sometimes the author wants the reader to have a specific perspective as well.
18. Ask: *What are the different feelings you get when reading a story in the first-person point of view versus the second-person point of view?* Discuss how different perspectives have different things to offer a narrative. The perspective from which a story is told has a great influence on how the reader feels while reading it.

With any time remaining, students can complete Fiction Fanatic Card (Handout 1.4) on *first-* and *second-person point of view*. Or, encourage students to think of an example and bring it in for the next lesson.

CLOSE

With any time remaining, students can complete Fiction Fanatic Card (Handout 1.4) on *first-* and *second-person point of view*. Or, encourage students to think of an example and bring it in for the next lesson.

HANDOUT 7.1

FIRST- AND SECOND-PERSON POINT OF VIEW

FIRST-PERSON SINGULAR POINT OF VIEW

I know I'm not an ordinary ten-year-old kid. I mean, sure, I do ordinary things. I eat ice cream. I ride my bike. I play ball. I have an XBox. Stuff like that makes me ordinary. I guess. And I feel ordinary. Inside.

—R. J. Palacio, *Wonder* (p.3)

The tooth was hanging by a thread. I could have reminded him that by the time I was in first grade I'd already lost three teeth. But I didn't.

—Judy Blume, *Cool Zone with the Pain and the Great One*

FIRST-PERSON PLURAL POINT OF VIEW

For as long as we could remember we had been together in the house which established the center of the known world. When we were younger we woke in the mornings while it was still dark.

—Joan Chase, *During the Reign of the Queen of Persia* (p. 49)

SECOND-PERSON POINT OF VIEW

Your heart races as you make your way through Snake Canyon, looking for the entrance to the Cave of Time. About midafternoon you reach the familiar grove of pine trees near the cave's entrance, only to find that landslides covered it over.

—Edward Packard, *Return to the Cave of Time* (p. 1)

HANDOUT 7.2

WHAT'S BEST FOR MY STORY?

Directions: Choosing a point of view influences the meaning of a story and the way it is perceived. What do you want the audience to understand better after reading your tale? Use the following sets of questions to help you think about what point of view you want to use to tell your story.

FIRST-PERSON POINT OF VIEW

1. Do I want the audience to be inside my head, seeing what I am observing and how?
2. *Main character*: Do I want the reader to understand me and what I am doing in the story from my own perspective?
3. *Observer*: Do I want to show the audience how I view someone or something else?

SECOND-PERSON POINT OF VIEW

1. Do I want the reader to feel like he or she is a part of the story?

THIRD-PERSON POINT OF VIEW

1. Do I want the reader to observe the story through an unknown narrator?
2. *Omniscient narrator*: Do I want the reader to have insight about what all of the characters are thinking and feeling?
3. *Limited narrator*: Do I want the reader to know what one character is thinking and feeling from an outside perspective?

LESSON 8 Point of View, Continued

MATERIALS

- Student writer's notebooks
- Student workshop folders
- Student copies of Chapter 1 (pp. 5–7, para. 4–13) from *Maniac Magee* by Jerry Spinelli (Little, Brown, 2014)
- Student copies of Chapter 1 (pp. 1–2, para. 1–3) from *The Giver* by Lois Lowry (HMH Books for Young Readers, 2014)
- Image: "Girl With Cat" (available at http://thegraphicsfairy.com/public-domain-download-girl-cat-sweet)
- Handout 1.4: Fiction Fanatic Card

- Literature is based on universal themes/characters/situations that embody the human experience and help us make sense of our own lives.
- Writers create stories to document and make sense of thoughts/feelings/understandings about themselves and the world around them.
- Different perspectives and opinions of an event are legitimate when justified by evidence.

OBJECTIVES

Students will:

- identify the narrator and point of view from which a fictional narrative is told,
- respond to a variety of prompts creatively and thoughtfully, and
- offer constructive criticism both verbally and in writing.

- Third-person point of view
- Omniscient narrator
- Limited narrator

SEQUENCE

ACTIVITY: WRITING WORKSHOP

1. Introduce the following prompt: *Choose either first- or second-person point of view. Describe a character from the point of view of another character.* Remind students that first-person narrators tell the story, and second-person narrators talk to the reader like the reader is a character in the story.
2. Ask students to respond to the prompt in their writer's notebooks. Give students 5–10 minutes before giving them a one-minute warning. Then, allow for 5–10 minutes of writing and/or transfer of writing to their workshop folders.
3. Ask students to form circle(s) (either as a full class or groups of 3–4) for the writers' retreat. Each student should read his or her prompt response aloud and allow time (about 2–3 minutes per response) for students to offer constructive feedback.
4. Encourage students to pay particular attention to the use of the point of view they chose (first or second person). Try to model constructive criticism by highlighting one common aspect of the writers' retreat to reinforce (e.g., a couple of great examples of using first- or second-person point of view).

INSTRUCTION: THIRD-PERSON POINT OF VIEW

5. Tell students: *During the writing workshop today, you wrote about first- and second-person narrators. Now, we are going to talk about third-person narrators. You will be in two groups for this activity. Each group will be thinking about the following questions:*
   - ✓ What pronouns does the narrator use?
   - ✓ Can we tell who the narrator is? Is he or she a character in the story or not?

6. Assign students to groups based on the results of Formative Assessment 2.

- **Group A** (0–5 answers correct on Formative Assessment 2) should read the excerpt from *The Giver* by Lois Lowry, which features a limited narrator.
- **Group B** (6–10 answers correct) should read the excerpt from *Maniac Magee* by Jerry Spinelli, which features an omniscient narrator.

7. Have each group record its responses to the questions on the board.
8. Afterward, review the answers. For pronouns, make sure you expand the list for any missing from the passage so you have *he, him, his, she, her, hers, they, them,* and *their*. In *Maniac Magee,* the narrator is not a character, but an outsider. We do not know who it is, but the narrator is able to tell us about the past and present. This means he or she is an *omniscient* or all-knowing narrator. In *The Giver,* the narrator is also an outsider, but he or she is telling us the story from Jonah's perspective, meaning we learn about everything he thinks and feels. This means he or she is a *limited* narrator.

The passage from *Maniac McGee* relates back to Claudia in *From the Mixed-Up Files of Mrs. Basil E. Frankweiler*. She only feels things are unfair because she doesn't know any better, but Maniac McGee actually lives in an unfortunate situation. Students can learn more about perspective, as the limited view we are given of Claudia and the omniscient view we are given of Maniac can make their situations seem more similar than they are.

The Giver excerpt can be used to address power—students can see that the characters are frightened because they don't have knowledge, and they have to wait for a powerful figure to give them information.

9. Add *third-person point of view* to the word wall.

ACTIVITY: POINT OF VIEW

10. Tell students they are going to revisit the image of the girl and the cat from Lesson 7. Display the image. Say: *We are going to be the narrator, and in this case, we are going to focus on the girl to limit our perspective. What would a third-person limited narrator say about what is happening? What if you limited your perspective to the other character in the picture?*
11. Choose 2–3 students to share. See if you get a variety of responses (singular, plural, main, observer). If not, prompt students to provide the other responses (e.g., *what would the sentence be if both the girl and the cat were narrators? What would the sentence be if the girl was an observer?).* Example sentences may include:
    - ✓ **Girl:** She was surprised to see the cat was waiting so patiently.
    - ✓ **Cat:** The cat looked longingly at the bowl and hoped that the girl would put it down soon.

12. Ask: *What would an omniscient narrator say about what is happening?* Remind students that *omniscient* means all knowing, so they can com-

ment on anything that is going on in the scene. If needed, prompt students with: *An omniscient narrator would know what both the cat and the girl are thinking—what would that sound like?* An example sentence may include: *The cat was angry that she would not set the bowl down, but the girl thought the cat was being patient.*

13. Ask: *Why do authors use different points of view?* Help students understand that the authors are trying to help us connect with the stories and characters. They should also understand that there is no "correct" point of view—they just help us connect in different ways. Let students drive this discussion, but guide them to the following conclusions:
    - ✓ **First-person narrators** create a personal connection with the main character(s), as the main character(s) is (are) talking to the reader.
    - ✓ **Second-person narrators** create an interactive connection, as they make the reader feel like he or she is part of the story.
    - ✓ **Third-person narrators** create a connection with the author, as it feels like the author is telling the reader about what is happening.

14. Say: *Think about what kind of writer you want to be, and why? Take about 5 minutes to write about what kind of narrator you want to use and why in your writer's notebook.*
15. After 5 minutes, allow students to share their responses if they wish. Discuss different perspectives on what kinds of writers students want to be and why. Let students know that each person has his or her own preference and reasoning, and that is okay.
16. (Optional) Divide students into heterogeneous small groups. Project the previous excerpts on the board and have students decide whether the passages are first-, second-, or third-person point of view. If you have time, you can bring in other texts students have read as well. Alternatively, you can group students according to books they love in common and have them make this decision.

Focus on the rubric: Display Appendix A5: Road to Publishing: Point of View. As a class, decide how the excerpt from *The Giver* fits into this rubric. The idea is to expose students to the rubric so they will understand it for their final stories later in the unit.

CLOSE

With any time remaining, students can complete Fiction Fanatic Card (Handout 1.4) on *third-person point of view*, *omniscient narrator*, and *limited narrator*. Or encourage students to think of an example and bring it in during the next lesson.

LESSON

9 Conflict

MATERIALS

- ✓ Student writer's notebooks
- ✓ Student workshop folders
- ✓ Teacher's copy of Chapter 1 (pp. 7–10, para. 1–20) from *A Wrinkle in Time* by Madeleine L'Engle (Square Fish, 2007; also available at http://www.npr.org/books/titles/146158461/a-wrinkle-in-time-50th-anniversary-edition#excerpt)
- ✓ Handout 1.4: Fiction Fanatic Card

- Literature is based on universal themes/characters/situations that embody the human experience and help us make sense of our own lives.
- Different perspectives and opinions of an event are legitimate when justified by evidence.

OBJECTIVES

Students will:

- ✓ recognize different forms of conflict in a fictional narrative, and
- ✓ identify the narrator and point of view from which a fictional narrative is told.

- Conflict

SEQUENCE

ACTIVITY: WRITING WORKSHOP

1. Introduce the following prompt: *Describe a character from the point of view of another character in third-person point of view.*

2. Ask students to respond to the prompt in their writer's notebooks. Give students 5–10 minutes before giving them a one-minute warning. Then, allow for 5–10 minutes of writing and/or transfer of writing to their workshop folders.
3. Ask students to form circle(s) (either as a full class or groups of 3–4) for the writers' retreat. Each student should read his or her prompt response aloud and allow time (about 2–3 minutes per response) for students to offer constructive feedback.
4. Encourage students to pay particular attention to incorporating the ideas of third-person point of view. Try to model constructive criticism by highlighting one common aspect of the writers' retreat to reinforce (e.g., see if you can add to the list of words that can replace "said"). Be sure to take note of any conflicts that may appear in students' work to use as a transition into conflict later on in the lesson.

INSTRUCTION: CONFLICT

5. Tell students: *Today, we are going to talk about something that appeared (or did not appear) in some of your responses today. It is an important part of both fiction and real life called conflict. What do you think about when you hear that word?*
6. Write students' responses on the board, and use these responses to create a class definition of *conflict*, which should address incompatibility or disagreement between people or things, particularly those that affect the plot.
7. Tell students that there are four major types of conflict, and ask if they can list them. If needed, display *man versus* _________ four times to guide students to the different types. Ask: *What conflicts do you think exist, or what conflicts do you already know about?*
8. Allow students to fill in the blanks and define the terms. Ask for examples of each. If they are stuck, provide some examples for them, but still have them define the terms and come up with additional examples:
   - ✓ **Man versus man:** External conflict between characters (e.g., the Rebellion v. the Dark Side in the *Star Wars* movies).
   - ✓ **Man versus nature:** External conflict between characters and natural events, like the weather (e.g., WALL-E v. Earth in *WALL-E*).
   - ✓ **Man versus self:** Internal conflict about what a character thinks/feels about him-/her-/itself (e.g., Elsa's feelings about her powers in *Frozen*).
   - ✓ **Man versus society:** External conflict between character(s) and organizations/beliefs (e.g., Katniss v. the Capitol in the *Hunger Games* series).

9. Add *conflict* to the word wall.

ACTIVITY: CONFLICT

10. Invite students to find a comfortable place for listening. Remind them that they will want to listen for different types of conflict.
11. Read the excerpt from *A Wrinkle in Time* by Madeleine L'Engle up to "Automatically she pushed her glasses into position, ran her fingers through her mouse-brown hair, so that it stood wildly on end, and let out a sigh almost as noisy as the wind."
12. Ask: *What examples of conflict do we see Meg Murry handle in this passage?* There are possible examples for all four types. Have students find at least one example of each. Explain that conflicts are not always small moments like in this excerpt. They can also be major parts of the story, like in some of the examples listed earlier.
13. Ask: *How do authors portray conflict? What kinds of words and sentences do they use?* Take note of the negative connotation of many of the words (e.g., afraid, wrong, scornfully, etc.) and how both dialogue and description help us see the conflicts.
14. Ask: *How might point of view change how we see a conflict?* Explain that it is easier for us to see internal conflict when we have first-person (main) or third-person narrators, who can give us insight into a person's thoughts and feelings. The perspective of the conflict might change with a different character as well. For example, Meg thinks that her mother is bothered by the gossip but doesn't show it, but she might not find it a conflict at all.

Focus on the rubric: Display Appendix A6: Road to Publishing: Conflict. As a class, decide how the excerpt from *A Wrinkle in Time* fits into this rubric. The idea is to expose students to the rubric so they will understand it for their final stories later in the unit.

With any time remaining, students can complete Fiction Fanatic Card (Handout 1.4) on *conflict*. Or, encourage students to think of an example and bring it in during the next lesson.

15. (Optional) Ask students to select one of the pieces in their workshop folders that they think might be a good start for their final fiction story. Remind students their ultimate product will be a story they will write, so tell them to be sure to select one they've gotten feedback on and that they think might be a great starting point for their story. They should then work on a revision of that piece.

LESSON 10

Audience

MATERIALS

- ✓ Student writer's notebooks
- ✓ Student workshop folders
- ✓ Handout 1.4: Fiction Fanatic Card

- Writers use senses, emotions, and images to evoke connections between the text and the reader.
- Different perspectives and opinions of an event are legitimate when justified by evidence.

OBJECTIVES

Students will:

- ✓ respond to a variety of prompts creatively and thoughtfully, and
- ✓ offer constructive criticism both verbally and in writing.

- Audience

SEQUENCE

ACTIVITY: WRITING WORKSHOP

1. Introduce the following prompt: *Without using dialogue, describe a conflict in 250–500 words that might occur during recess.*
2. Ask students to respond to the prompt in their writer's notebooks. Give students 5–10 minutes before giving them a one-minute warning. Then, allow for 5–10 minutes of writing and/or transfer of writing to their workshop folders.

3. Ask students to form circle(s) (either as a full class or groups of 3–4) for the writers' retreat. Each student should read his or her prompt response aloud and allow time (about 2–3 minutes per response) for students to offer constructive feedback.
4. Encourage students to pay particular attention to developing their conflict. Try to model constructive criticism by highlighting one common aspect of the writers' retreat to reinforce (e.g., a good example of a particular kind of conflict). Try to model constructive criticism by highlighting one common aspect of the writers' retreat to reinforce (e.g., see if you can add to the list of words that can replace "said.")

INSTRUCTION: AUDIENCE

5. Tell students that, so far, the class has been the audience for their writing. Ask them to think about how changing their audience might change how they think about their writing. For example, many of the excerpts they have read during the unit are written for children. The authors' choices for point of view, type of conflict, setting, and characters are all influenced by the audience. Ask:
   - ✓ *Think about what we've read during this unit. Do we notice any patterns with setting?* Students may note that schools or homes appear often. Point out that some readers may find a certain type of setting more appealing than others and will read more books that take place in farms rather than cities, for example.
   - ✓ *Do you find yourself reading more fiction that resembles the place where you live, or do you prefer other places?* Regardless of whether or not we are drawn to places similar or different from our own, where we live has an influence on our choices.
   - ✓ *Do we notice any patterns with characters?* Students should note they are all close in age to the audience's age, or younger.
   - ✓ *Why are students your age drawn to books with this type of character?* Students should conclude that it makes it easier to connect with people that way.
   - ✓ *Do we notice any patterns with point of view?* Most examples are first person or third-person limited, so that we can better understand the thoughts and feelings of the characters.
   - ✓ *Are there any patterns in conflict?* Think about some of the literature we've used in our Fiction Fanatics Cards. There is a variety presented, but the fewest involve man versus nature thus far—however, it is hard to make conclusions about that based on small excerpts, which you should point out to students.

✓ *How has our audience influenced what we wrote?* Think about how changing the audience might change how we think of a story. For example, the audiences for *Star Wars* films are science fiction fans, which can be seen in its setting (in the future and in space) and fantastical creatures and robots (like Chewbacca and BB-8). It also has elements that may appeal to a more general audience like romance, family, and adventure.

ACTIVITY: AUDIENCE

6. Ask students to choose a workshop response from those they have previously completed and rewrite it with a new audience in mind.

2E

- If you have students who cannot understand the concept of anyone having a different point of view, give them the option of rewriting a prompt to fit the audience they want even more clearly.
- For students who struggle with writing, encourage them to choose a shorter prompt response to alter.

PREPARATION: FORMATIVE ASSESSMENT 3

7. Collect students' responses to this lesson's writing workshop and use them to inform the choices for the writing workshop in Lesson 11, or ask students where they feel they need more practice and have them write it on an Exit Card.

With any time remaining, students can complete Fiction Fanatic Card (Handout 1.4) on *audience*. Or, encourage students to think of an example and bring it in during the next lesson.

LESSON 11

Plot

MATERIALS

- Student writer's notebooks
- Student workshop folders
- Teacher's copy of "The Queen Bee" by the Brothers Grimm (available at http://www.gutenberg.org/files/19068/19068-h/19068-h.htm#illus-291)
- Handout 11.1: Brainstorming
- Handout 11.2: Plot Diagram
- Handout 11.3: Application Extension
- Appendix A7: Writing Prompt Bank
- Appendix A8: Road to Publishing: Plot

Literature is based on universal themes/characters/situations that embody the human experience and help us make sense of our own lives.

OBJECTIVES

Students will:

- use brainstorming to generate ideas at the prewriting stage of composition,
- use analysis skills to organize thoughts through prewriting, AND
- identify specific steps commonly used in the writing process including prewriting, drafting, editing, revising, and publishing.

- Plot
- Exposition
- Rising action
- Turning point
- Falling action
- Denouement

SEQUENCE

ACTIVITY: WRITING WORKSHOP

1. Tell students: *Today, you are going to think about the setting, characters, conflicts, and other story elements that complement each other to create a complete short story. You can include elements that you wrote about previously from your writer's notebook or workshop folder, or you can write about something completely new.*

This writing workshop will help students begin planning their final stories. They will think about the audience, setting, characters, etc., that they want to write about. Remind students to be thinking about topics and characters that interest them or that they are passionate about.

2. Have students complete Handout 11.1: Brainstorming.
3. For the writing prompt, provide each student with a prompt (see Appendix A7: Writing Prompt Bank) based on Formative Assessment 3. If a student does not have a clear area of weakness to focus on, choose a writing prompt based on the student's informal self-evaluation of where he or she feels he or she needs more practice.
4. After you have seen each student's brainstorming handout, give students 5–10 minutes to respond to their prompt before giving them a one-minute warning. Then, ask them to form circle(s) with their group for the writers' retreat.
5. As a class or in small groups (3–4 students), have each student read his or her prompt response aloud, and allow time (about 2–3 minutes per response) for students to offer constructive feedback. The retreat should not dominate the lesson.

INSTRUCTION: PLOT

6. Tell students that before they focus on writing their complete stories, there's one more thing they need to talk about—plot. Ask: *What is plot?* Students should understand that plot is what happens in a story.
7. Say: *One way to think about plot is by using a plot diagram. A plot diagram is a way to picture a story on a graph. What do you think a plot diagram looks like?* Let students make some guesses. If students do not know what a plot diagram is, draw one for them (see Handout 11.2).

Leave blanks/underlined spaces for each of the plot diagram labels. Have students guess what the terms might be that fill in the blanks. Guide students to the following elements and definitions on the plot diagram:

- ✓ **Exposition:** Introduction, what we need to know to understand the major conflict in the story.
- ✓ **Rising action:** Parts of the story that explain how the major conflict impacts the characters, setting, etc.
- ✓ **Turning point (climax):** Where the major conflict occurs.
- ✓ **Falling action:** How characters handle the major conflict.
- ✓ **Denouement:** Ending, how the major conflict is resolved.

8. Add *plot* to the word wall.
9. Explain to students that the length of the lines in the plot diagram depends on the amount of time spent on each segment in the story itself. For example, if there is more rising action, and it all happens very quickly, that line would be long and steep. Not all lines for each element of the plot diagram will be equal in length; the length changes depending on the story.

ACTIVITY: PLOT

10. Tell students: *Let's read a short story and see if we can apply this simple plot diagram to the story.* Display "The Queen Bee" by the Brothers Grimm, and invite students to find a comfortable place to listen.
11. Remind students that they will want to listen for all the parts of a plot. Let them know they can take notes as they read to help them keep track of each part of the plot. Read the excerpt out loud to students. When you finish, have students look at the excerpt one more time.
12. Distribute Handout 11.2: Plot Diagram. As a class, label each part of the story based on the traditional plot diagram.

Focus on the rubric: Display Appendix A8: Road to Publishing: Plot. As a class, decide how "The Queen Bee" fits into this rubric. The idea is to expose students to the rubric so they will understand it for their final stories.

13. Then, ask students to use the basic plot diagram structure to map out their story's plot in their writer's notebooks. They should draw the length of each line in the diagram for each plot element as they see fit.
14. Give students time to begin developing their plot ideas. Encourage them to revisit Handout 11.1: Brainstorming to help them. They should be ready to share their plot diagrams at the beginning of the next lesson.

15. Visit with students. If a student's story looks like it is too complicated to complete in a reasonable amount of time, encourage him or her to narrow the focus.

We suggest adding this activity if students have mastered the concepts thus far.

ACTIVITY: APPLICATION EXTENSION

16. (Optional) Ask: *What if we also wanted to include how our thoughts and feelings about the story change as the story goes on? Let's think about a different kind of graph to help us see that.*
17. Display and distribute Handout 11.3: Application Extension. Draw out how you see "The Queen Bee" unfolding in terms of good/bad events. If students disagree with you, remind them of the importance of perspective. Use a different color to make their changes so the class can see how perspective can change the understanding of the plot.
18. Ask: *Are there any other ways we can graph a story*? Let a few students share their ideas.
19. Have students work on the plot of their stories in their writer's notebooks, choosing one of the following options:
    - ✓ **Practical:** Use the basic structure of the plot diagram, but draw the length of each line in the diagram for every plot element as you see fit.
    - ✓ **Analytical:** Graph the plot using the beginning/end as the X-axis and good/bad as the Y-axis.
    - ✓ **Creative:** Graph the plot using an X- and Y-axis of your own creation.

Kurt Vonnegut created this type of graph in his master's thesis at the University of Chicago. He felt that main characters' actions could be graphed to reveal the events of a story. Vonnegut often discussed his idea in lectures on creative writing (see this article in *The Washington Post* for more details: https://www.washingtonpost.com/news/wonk/wp/2015/02/09/kurt-vonnegut-graphed-the-worlds-most-popular-stories).

Each activity is one of the three types of intelligences from Sternberg's (1986) Triarchic Theory of Intelligence. Activities based in each of the three categories of this model should include the following:

- **Practical:** Students apply, use, or implement to better understand a concept or skill.
- **Analytic:** Students critique, evaluate, or assess to better understand a concept or skill.
- **Creative:** Students invent, discover, imagine, or predict to better understand a concept or skill.

Name: ______________________________ Date: ____________

HANDOUT 11.1

BRAINSTORMING

Directions: Think about your final story. Use the chart below to brainstorm about the setting, characters, conflicts, and other story elements.

Setting	
Characters	
Protagonist:	**Antagonist:**
Stock Characters:	
Point of View	
Major Conflict(s)	

HANDOUT 11.2

PLOT DIAGRAM

Directions: Label each part of the plot diagram with the events from "The Queen Bee" by the Brothers Grimm.

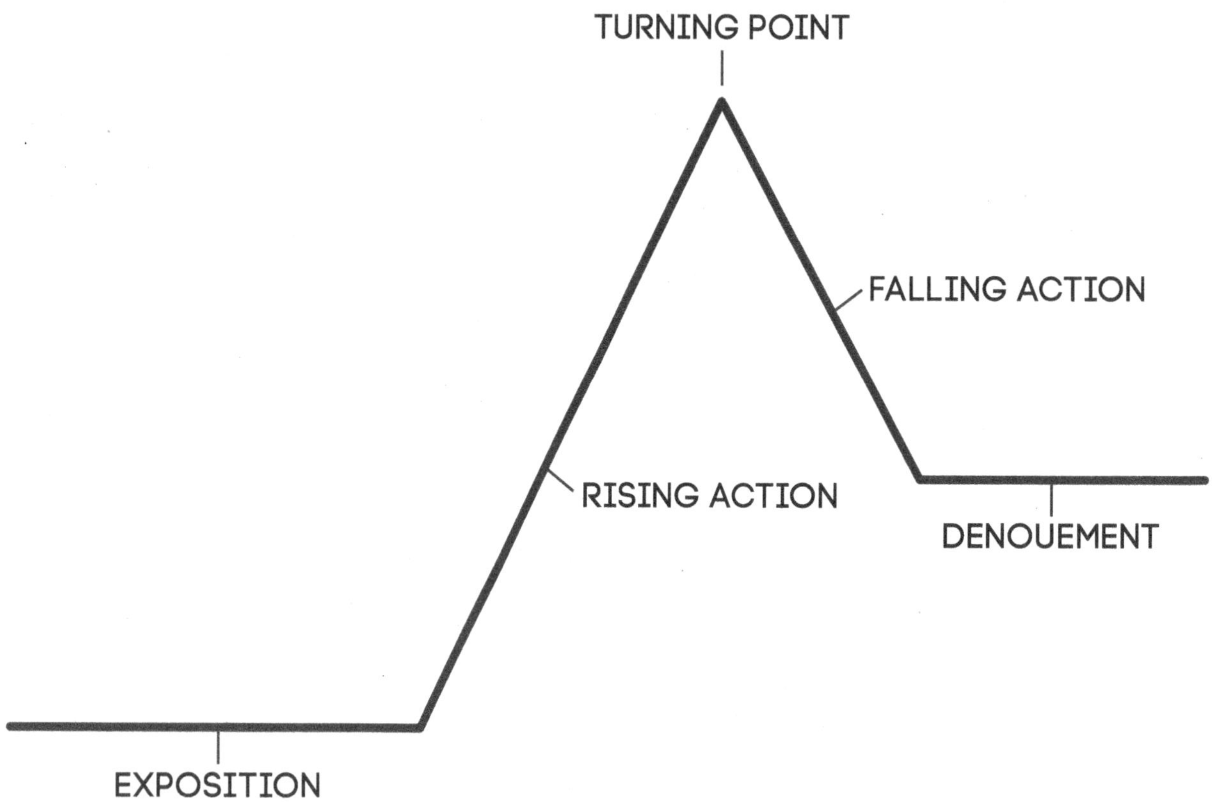

Name: ______________________________ **Date:** ______________

HANDOUT 11.3

APPLICATION EXTENSION

Directions: Choose a character from "The Queen Bee" and decide how the story unfolds in terms of good events (for example, good things that happened to the character) and bad events. For each point you create on the graph, write a few words about the event it represents.

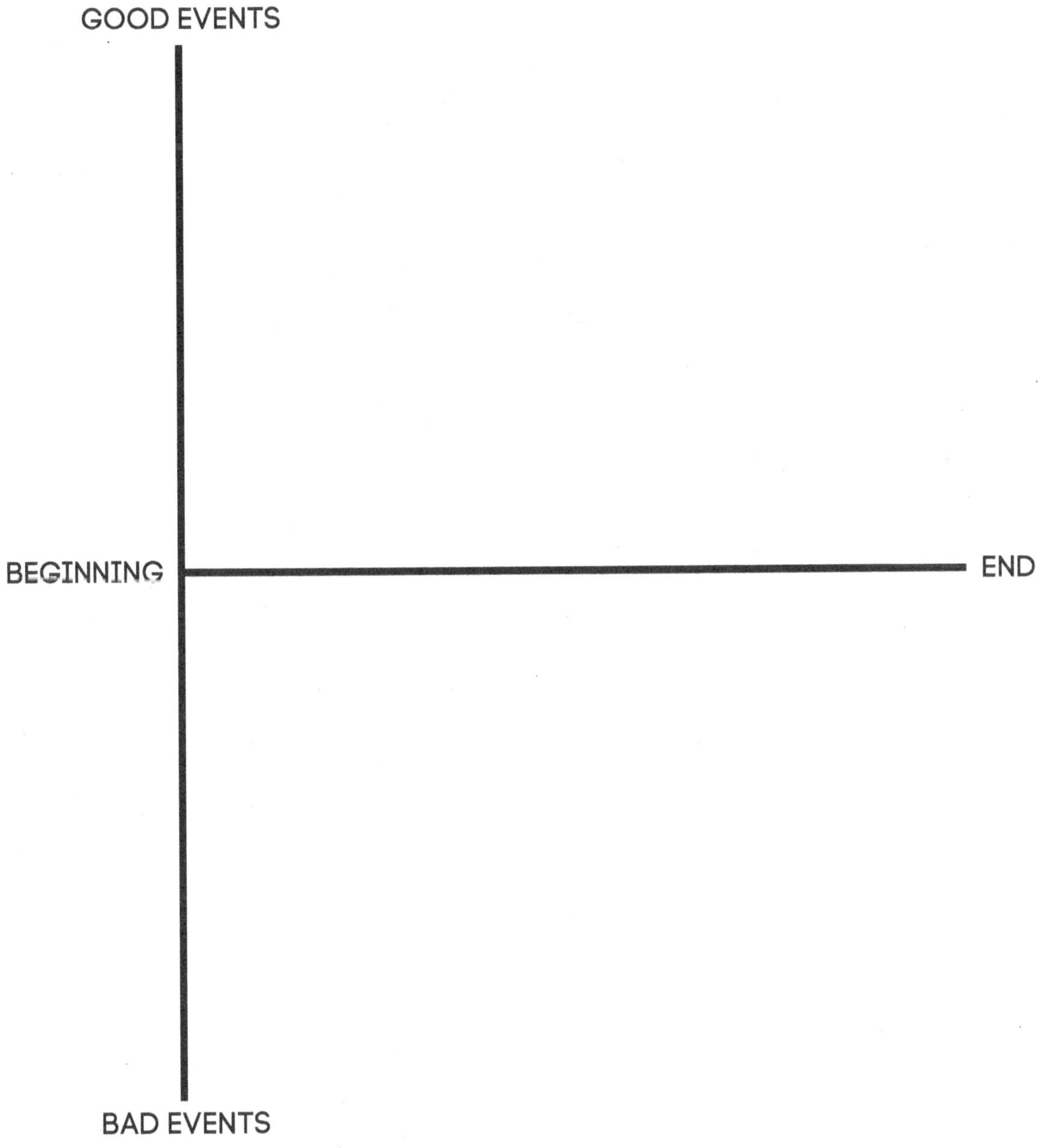

LESSON

12 Openings

MATERIALS

- ✓ Student writer's notebooks
- ✓ Teacher's copy of Chapter 1 (pp. 1–3) from *Walk Two Moons* by Sharon Creech (HarperCollins, 2011; also available at http://www.npr.org/books/titles/205462786/walk-two-moons#excerpt)
- ✓ Handout 12.1: Road to Publishing: Final Story Assignment
- ✓ Handout 12.2: Your Editor Says . . . Rubric
- ✓ Handout 12.3: Road to Publishing: Self-Edit
- ✓ Handout 12.4: Road to Publishing: Peer Edit

Writers use senses, emotions, and images to evoke connections between the text and the reader.

OBJECTIVES

Students will:

- ✓ use different story devices to enrich narrative writing,
- ✓ engage the reader with sentence and word variety, and
- ✓ demonstrate knowledge of the fiction genre by writing and presenting an original fictional narrative.

- Opening

SEQUENCE

ACTIVITY: WRITING WORKSHOP

1. As a class or in small groups (3–4 students), have each student share their plot diagram, and allow time (about 2–3 minutes per response) for students to offer constructive feedback. Encourage students to pay particular attention to each component of their developing plot. Try to model constructive criticism by highlighting one common aspect of the writers' retreat to reinforce (e.g., a good example of a diagram that includes clear events for each aspect of plot).

INSTRUCTION: OPENINGS

2. Tell students that as they work on their stories, one of the most important things will be the beginning. They need to hook their readers and get them interested so they will want to read more. To better understand this, students will look at the opening of a novel to see what techniques they might want to emulate.
3. Invite students to find a comfortable place to listen to an excerpt from *Walk Two Moons* by Sharon Creech. Remind them that they will want to listen for anything that catches their attention, particularly related to the author's use of characterization, setting, and imagery. Read it out loud to students. When you finish, tell them to take a moment to look at it again.

"Don't judge a man until you've walked two moons in his moccasins" is a proverb believed to have been used by American Indians. It has become a saying in modern culture, partly because of its use in the title of this novel. Sharon Creech said she found it in a Chinese fortune cookie.

In her acceptance of the Newbery Medal she referenced the saying:

> I saw an invitation, from characters to writer, and from writer to reader: come along and walk with us awhile, slip into our moccasins so that you might see what we think and feel, and so that you might understand why we do what we do, and so that you might glimpse the larger world outside your own. . . . Every book implicitly offers this invitation, and every book offers a journey, whether it is a literal one, a metaphorical one, or both. (as cited in Roberts, 2008)

Consider sharing this quote with students as they start down the final path on the Road to Publishing.

In this story, the character explores the idea of place when readers see that she misses her rural home. Missing home, especially if students have also moved from a rural area, may be something that some students can connect with.

4. Ask: *How does the author use characterization, setting, and imagery? How many of you want to read more of this story?* Hopefully most students want to read more, but some may not. This is a valid opinion.
5. Ask: *Why do some people read the first few pages and don't want to go on, and some do? Does that make it a bad book?* Help students understand that not all books appeal to all everyone. Explain that when students write their own short stories, not everyone will like it, and that is okay. It is more important to write something they are proud of.
6. Form students into two groups:
   - ✓ **Group A:** Students who do want to read more of *Walk Two Moons* should brainstorm a list of what makes them want to read more.
   - ✓ **Group B:** Students who did not want to read more of *Walk Two Moons* should brainstorm a list of what they thought was missing.

   If all students fall into the same group, challenge your students who do better with point of view/perspective to think about how students on the opposite side would think about the text (e.g., if they all wanted to read on, challenge some students to think about why some students may not want to read more).
7. Have both groups share their lists with the entire class. As groups share, make sure students also understand the author's use of characterization/setting/metaphor, but explain that it is okay if not everyone finds it interesting.
8. (Optional) Consider sharing with students some other examples of great opening lines for further inspiration. Some great resources include:
   - ✓ https://www.theguardian.com/childrens-books-site/2016/jan/01/best-opening-lines-childrens-and-young-adult-fiction
   - ✓ http://www.shortlist.com/entertainment/literatures-greatest-opening-paragraphs
   - ✓ http://review.gawker.com/the-50-best-first-sentences-in-fiction-1665532271
   - ✓ http://www.barnesandnoble.com/blog/teen/15-of-the-best-opening-lines-in-ya

> Students can use regular paper, their writer's notebooks, or even poster paper to write down their list as they brainstorm. Each group member should be ready to share examples with the class.

INSTRUCTION: FINAL STORY ASSIGNMENT

9. Tell students they will begin working on a draft of their stories. They should include all of the elements they have learned about (i.e., alignment, character, conflict, dialogue, imagery, plot, point of view, and setting). They may work on it in class or at home, but the goal is to give them enough time in class to finish during the next few lessons.
10. Distribute Handout 12.1: Road to Publishing: Final Story Assignment and Handout 12.2: Your Editor Says . . . Rubric. Give students a few min-

utes to review the handouts on their own. Then, review each component as a class. Make sure you mention the class anthology (a collection of all students' work) and the Author Event (where students will be able to talk about their stories).

11. Tell students they are already on their way to becoming published authors, but that the rubric will help them check for key elements in their writing as they work their way toward a final product. They have already had some practice on each element, but the final story is about bringing all of those pieces together.

INSTRUCTION: FINAL STORY EDITING PROCESS

12. Remind students that authors always need to edit their work before they publish. Distribute Handout 12.3: Road to Publishing: Self-Edit and Handout 12.4: Road to Publishing: Peer Edit.

Based on their most recent work, pair students for peer editing who are at a similar level in their writing. This will make the feedback process more useful to all students.

13. Explain to students that they will go through all of the steps on Handout 12.1 over the next few lessons in preparation for the Author Event. You (or the students) will invite other teachers, administrators, parents, grandparents, guardians, etc., to the event. Students will set their books up in the classroom for viewing by the guests and their classmates. Each student will be able to talk with interested readers and answer questions about their work.

PREPARATION: FORMATIVE ASSESSMENT 4

14. At the end of the lesson, collect all students' work on their final stories so far. Review them in order to place students into groups by interest for the next lesson on genre. Continue to review student work if students choose to work on their final stories for homework.

HANDOUT 12.1

ROAD TO PUBLISHING: FINAL STORY ASSIGNMENT

Directions: You have been practicing, brainstorming, and plotting . . . now it is time to finish the journey by publishing your work through our class publication company. You will be published once you submit your work to the editor (your teacher). Your work will be published in our Class Anthology, and you will have an opportunity to present it at our Author Event!

A publication company is in charge of distributing the author's work. Some famous companies are Scholastic, Random House, HarperCollins, and Oxford University Press. Bring ideas about what to name the class publication company to the next lesson.

WRITING AND EDITING PROCESS

As you have traveled down this road, you have looked at:

- Imagery
- Setting
- Characters
- Characterization
- Dialogue
- Point of view
- Conflict
- Plot
- Publication details

To write your final story, you are going to put all these elements together into one coherent narrative.

1. To create that narrative, you should write, edit, and revise until you are confident that every element meets the publication requirements on Handout 12.2: Your Editor Says . . . Rubric.

HANDOUT 12.1, CONTINUED

2. The editing process starts with writing the first draft. Don't worry too much about what it looks like—as the famous author William Faulkner said, "Get it down. Take chances. It may be bad, but it's the only way you can do anything really good."
3. Then you will complete a self-edit, and make changes based on Handout 12.2: Road to Publishing: Self-Edit.
4. After these changes, you will be assigned a peer editor to assist you, and then make changes based on the Handout 12.3: Road to Publishing: Peer Edit. that he or she completes.
5. Finally, you will look over Handout 12.2: Your Editor Says . . . Rubric one last time, and make your final submission to your editor, who will help you prepare your manuscript for publication in the Class Anthology.

So go forth and write something that is important to you! As Virginia Woolf says, "So long as you write what you wish to write, that is all that matters."

HANDOUT 12.2

YOUR EDITOR SAYS . . . RUBRIC

Element	You need to go back to the drawing board . . .	You need multiple revisions . . .	You need one more revision . . .	Your work is publishable!
Alignment (*Note.* "Story elements" refers to all of the elements listed below.)	None of the story elements are consistent or make sense.	Some of the story elements are consistent and make sense.	Most of the story elements are consistent and make sense.	All the story elements are consistent and make sense.
Characters (*Note.* Stock characters are not required.)	There are no characters developed enough to be a protagonist/antagonist/stock character.	The protagonist/antagonist are underdeveloped. The stock character serves no purpose.	The protagonist/antagonist are identifiable. The stock character has a debatable purpose.	The protagonist/antagonist are well-developed. The stock character serves a clear purpose.
Characterization	Either direct or indirect characterization is missing.	There is an uneven balance between direct and indirect characterization that is distracting to the reader.	The direct and/or indirect characterization is developed but inconsistent.	Both direct and indirect characterization is consistent and well-developed.
Conflict	There is no major conflict.	The major conflict is unclear.	The major conflict is identifiable.	The major conflict is clearly identifiable and well-developed.
Dialogue	There is no dialogue, even when it would be relevant.	There is dialogue, but there are issues with punctuation and/or flow (e.g., it is difficult to tell who is speaking).	The dialogue does not seem authentic to the characters (e.g., the way the characters speak does not match their characterization).	The dialogue flows well and is authentic to the characters.

HANDOUT 12.2, CONTINUED

Element	You need to go back to the drawing board . . .	You need multiple revisions . . .	You need one more revision . . .	Your work is publishable!
Imagery	There is no imagery.	The imagery is confusing and does not seem related to story elements.	The imagery does not always fit with the other story elements.	The imagery fits well with the other story elements.
Plot	The plot is hard to follow.	There are gaps in the plot.	There are minor points of confusion in the plot.	The plot is clear and easy to follow.
Point of View	The point of view switches narrators at random.	The point of view is inconsistent and confusing at times.	The point of view is clear, although there are minor issues with consistency.	The point of view is clear and consistent.
Publication Details (title, title page, biography, dedication)	The publication elements are missing or completely incorrect.	The publication elements are incorrect.	The publication elements are misleading (inconsistent between content of story and what is presented).	The publication elements are clearly marketing the story appropriately.
Setting	The setting is never clarified.	There are missing details about the setting without a reason.	Some details of the setting are inconsistent.	The setting is clear and consistent.

HANDOUT 12.3

ROAD TO PUBLISHING: SELF-EDIT

Element	Yes	No	Evidence and/or Ideas for Revisions
Alignment All of the story elements (listed below) are consistent and make sense.	❑	❑	
Characters The protagonist and antagonist are well-developed. The stock character serves a clear purpose. (*Note:* Stock characters are not required.)	❑	❑	
Characterization Both direct and indirect characterization are consistent and well-developed.	❑	❑	
Conflict The major conflict(s) is/are clearly identifiable and well-developed.	❑	❑	
Dialogue The dialogue flows well and is authentic to the characters.	❑	❑	

HANDOUT 12.3, CONTINUED

Element	Yes	No	Evidence and/or Ideas for Revisions
Imagery The imagery fits well with the other story elements.	❑	❑	
Plot The plot is clear and easy to follow.	❑	❑	
Point of View The point of view is clear and consistent.	❑	❑	
Publication Details The publication elements are clearly marketing the story appropriately.	❑	❑	
Setting The setting is clear and consistent.	❑	❑	

HANDOUT 12.4

ROAD TO PUBLISHING: PEER EDIT

Element	Needs Work	Good	Excellent	Evidence and/or Revision Suggestions
Alignment All of the story elements (listed below) are consistent and make sense.	❑	❑	❑	
Characters The protagonist and antagonist are well-developed. The stock character serves a clear purpose. (*Note.* Stock characters are not required.)	❑	❑	❑	
Characterization Both direct and indirect characterization are consistent and well-developed.	❑	❑	❑	
Conflict The major conflict(s) is/are clearly identifiable and well-developed.	❑	❑	❑	
Dialogue The dialogue flows well and is authentic to the characters.	❑	❑	❑	

HANDOUT 12.4, CONTINUED

Element	Needs Work	Good	Excellent	Evidence and/or Revision Suggestions
Imagery The imagery fits well with the other story elements.	❑	❑	❑	
Plot The plot is clear and easy to follow.	❑	❑	❑	
Point of View The point of view is clear and consistent.	❑	❑	❑	
Publication Details The publication elements are clearly marketing the story appropriately.	❑	❑	❑	
Setting The setting is clear and consistent.	❑	❑	❑	

LESSON 13 Published Works and Genres

MATERIALS

- Student writer's notebooks
- Student workshop folders
- Selection of books
- Handout 12.1: Road to Publishing: Final Story Assignment
- Handout 13.1: Genre Guide

- Writers create stories to document and make sense of thoughts/feelings/understandings about themselves and the world around them.
- Writers use senses, emotions, and images to evoke connections between the text and the reader.

OBJECTIVES

Students will:

- identify and use the elements of a published work of fiction, including the story itself, title, title page, dedication, and biography;
- identify different characteristics in a fictional narrative in order to categorize the story by genre;
- use different story devices to enrich narrative writing;
- demonstrate knowledge of the fiction genre by writing and presenting an original fictional narrative; and
- produce and submit a final fictional narrative for publication using the elements of a story, including the title, title page, dedication, and biography.

- Genre

This activity can be combined with the second activity (group genre study) in this lesson. To combine these two activities, set up the genre group activity as stations first. Have students go to their station and examine the book(s) at the station for story elements. Then, share story elements as a class.

SEQUENCE

INSTRUCTION: PUBLISHED WORKS

1. Tell students: *You are all on your way to writing proper stories. What are some details common to published works (for example, how they all have title pages) that we can add to our stories to make them resemble published works? Let's each grab a book and make a list.*
2. Students should brainstorm story elements either individually, in pairs, or in small groups (depending on your class size and time available for this activity).
3. One students have brainstormed a list of elements they see in the published works, share and brainstorm a final list of published works elements as a class. Make sure that students note the following elements:
   - ✓ title,
   - ✓ title page,
   - ✓ dedication, and
   - ✓ biography.

If students really want to design covers for their stories, they can do so outside of class. Time in class should be spent working on writing.

4. Ask: *Why are these elements important?* They catch the reader's attention and help the author recruit the right audience. *Do these elements connect to setting, conflict, plot, or anything else we have talked about?* Yes. Sometimes the imagery the author uses is captured on the cover, and characters are often represented as described. Explain: *Although the cover matches story elements, authors do not create their own covers. The publisher usually creates these. For this reason, we are not going to be designing covers in class.*
5. Remind students that the publisher is the company that distributes the author's work. On Handout 12.1, they were asked to bring potential names for the class's publishing house. Have students vote on their favorite suggestion.
6. Although students will not create a copyright page, it is important that they understand the meaning and importance of it in works of fiction. Tell students that the copyright page makes the document official. A copyright means that the author or publisher owns the rights to the story. Some stories are free (e.g., *Alice's Adventures in Wonderland* and *Peter Pan*), because they are no longer under copyright. But readers have to pay for the books that are still protected by copyright.
7. The dedication and biography provide information about the author, which gives readers insight into the why the author chose to write about certain types of characters, settings, etc.

INSTRUCTION: GENRE

8. Tell students that before they begin working on their stories, you want them to consider one last element: *genre.*
9. Discuss the definitions of different types of genres, including adventure, comedy, fantasy, historical fiction, mystery, realistic fiction, and science fiction (see Handout 13.1). Make sure sctudents understand that genre is not only a way of categorizing literature after a work is published, but also can and does guide the creation of the story itself.
10. Add *genre* to the word wall.

ACTIVITY: GROUP GENRE STUDY

11. Distribute Handout 13.1: Genre Guide. Based on the results of Formative Assessment 4 and the genres of their stories, divide students into genre study groups. If students feel that, as they have started work on their story, they would rather move toward a different genre, then they can self-select to move to a different group. Students will be working in their groups to discuss key elements that fit their selected genre as they complete the handout.

> This activity can also be done in stations (see previous Tip Box). Distribute Handout 13.1: Genre Guide to stations, as well as books that fit each genre (see "Genre Study Book List" by ReadWriteThink for ideas http://www.readwritethink.org/files/resources/lesson_images/lesson270/genre_books.pdf).

12. As students discuss and brainstorm common elements of their stories, guide students to possible elements, such as:
    - ✓ adventure stories typically include (a) a character embarking on a journey or quest, (b) action and/or danger, and (c) an unusual setting or atypical location; and
    - ✓ comedies typically include (a) stock characters or a typical setting, (b) funny events and/or situations, (c) a happy ending.

    Visit "Genre Characteristics" by ReadWriteThink (http://www.readwritethink.org/files/resources/lesson_images/lesson270/genre_sheet.pdf) for more possible key elements of each genre.
13. Once each group has generated a list of key elements for its genre, remind students to keep these elements in mind throughout the final discussion. Have students keep Handout 13.1 in their workshop folders.

CLOSE

14. Ask: *How do authors use the literary elements we have discussed (imagery, characters, etc.) to make the genre clear to the reader?* (They make them authentic to the genre. For example, the imagery, characters, setting, etc., in realistic fiction are similar to things seen in real life. In fantasy, the imagery, characters, setting, etc., are very different from real life.)

15. Explain: *Remember how we talked about published works earlier in this lesson? Some of you may have chosen to design a cover on your own. Remember that the cover design might include setting and characters, but overall, the cover will usually also reveal the genre in some way.*
16. Allow students time to work on their stories for the rest of the lesson.

HANDOUT 13.1

GENRE GUIDE

Directions: Work with your group to discuss key elements and examples of your selected genre:

- **Adventure:** Stories about events that happen outside the characters' ordinary lives, usually involving danger and action.
- **Comedy:** Stories that are light, humorous, or satirical and have a happy resolution.
- **Fantasy:** Stories with fanciful or supernatural elements.
- **Historical Fiction:** Stories about fictional characters/events in a historical setting.
- **Mystery:** Stories that involve solving a crime or mysterious event.
- **Realistic Fiction:** Stories about events and characters that are true to life.
- **Science Fiction:** Stories that are fanciful but based on speculative scientific discoveries, environmental changes, space travel, or life on other planets.

Genre: ______________________________	
Key Element:	**Examples:**
Key Element:	**Examples:**
Key Element:	**Examples:**

LESSON 14 Final Story Workshops

Teacher's Note: Provide students with at least three more writing workshops to complete their stories. Depending upon where your students are in the process, they may need more time.

MATERIALS

- ✓ Student writer's notebooks
- ✓ Student workshop folders
- ✓ Handout 12.1: Road to Publishing: Final Story Assignment
- ✓ Handout 12.2: Your Editor Says . . . Rubric
- ✓ Handout 12.3: Road to Publishing: Self-Edit
- ✓ Handout 12.4: Road to Publishing: Peer Edit

- Literature is based on universal themes/characters/situations that embody the human experience and help us make sense of our own lives.
- Writers create stories to document and make sense of thoughts/feelings/understandings about themselves and the world around them.
- Writers use senses, emotions, and images to evoke connections between the text and the reader.
- Different perspectives and opinions of an event are legitimate when justified by evidence.

OBJECTIVES

Students will:

- ✓ use different story devices to enrich narrative writing,
- ✓ engage the reader with sentence and word variety,
- ✓ demonstrate knowledge of the fiction genre by writing and presenting an original fictional narrative,
- ✓ identify the elements of story structure in a fictional narrative,
- ✓ recognize different forms of conflict in a fictional narrative, and
- ✓ use evidence from text to support opinions.

SEQUENCE

You don't need to use the column format if you have different method of tracking student progress. The important thing is to make sure there is a visual way for both you and students to track their progress.

ACTIVITY: WRITING WORKSHOP

1. Have students work toward completing their stories in preparation for the Author Event. To keep track of students' progress, consider creating a progress board with the following categories each listed in a separate column:
   - ✓ First Draft,
   - ✓ Self-Edit,
   - ✓ Second Draft,
   - ✓ Peer Edit,
   - ✓ Final Draft, and
   - ✓ Publication.

   Each student should have a card with his or her name on it that can be moved from column to column as progress is made in writing his or her final story. When students want to move their name into the next column (i.e., the next step on the list), they should bring you their work so you can see what they have done and provide one-on-one feedback.
2. Review the final story writing steps with students again and the rubric (see Handouts 12.1 and 12.2). Be sure students know what they need to do to complete their stories, including how to self- and peer edit their works (see Handouts 12.3 and 12.4).

Try to pair students for peer editing who are at a similar level in their writing. This will make the feedback process more useful to all students.

PREPARATION: FOR NEXT LESSON

3. Make sure that you have plans in place to create the class anthology. Considerations may include whether you would like an artistically inclined student to create a cover, or have students vote on a picture that they feel represents their class.
4. Ensure guests are invited to the Author Event and that each student has an area to display his or her work.

LESSON 15 Publication and Author Event

MATERIALS

- ✓ Teacher's copies of Handout 12.2: Your Editor Says . . . Rubric

- Literature is based on universal themes/characters/situations that embody the human experience and help us make sense of our own lives.
- Writers create stories to document and make sense of thoughts/feelings/understandings about themselves and the world around them.
- Writers use senses, emotions, and images to evoke connections between the text and the reader.
- Different perspectives and opinions of an event are legitimate when justified by evidence.

OBJECTIVES

Students will:

- ✓ use different story devices to enrich narrative writing,
- ✓ engage the reader with sentence and word variety,
- ✓ demonstrate knowledge of the fiction genre by writing and presenting an original fictional narrative,
- ✓ identify the elements of story structure in a fictional narrative,
- ✓ recognize different forms of conflict in a fictional narrative, and
- ✓ use evidence from text to support opinions.

SEQUENCE

1. Have students set their stories up in the classroom for the Author Event. Students should have space where they are behind the desk next to their stories, so that interested readers can come over and ask them questions. Either (1) invite other classes, teachers, administrators, parents, etc., to come and talk with the authors, or (2) have the class split into

Make sure students all have the opportunity to get their stories bound—either using brads, plastic sleeves, or even a spiral binding. We suggest having students complete this process in class so that all the stories will be at a similar level of "publishing" or production for the Author Event. Remember, it is the quality of the writing rather than the production aesthetics that are important.

Consider having students submit their work for real-world publication. Several publishers accept student work. Check out The Telling Room's list at http://www.tellingroom.org/get-published/places-publish.

two groups—one half will be authors and one half will be readers. If you choose Option 2, make sure students switch roles halfway through class so everyone gets to be an author.

2. Collect students' final stories to create a class anthology of short stories to either display in the classroom or in the library. Be sure to make copies so you can still score students' work using the Fiction Rubric.

Unit 2
Memories, Memoir, and Me

BACKGROUND

Memories, Memoir, and Me is a curriculum unit designed for students to explore a variety of nonfiction texts with a focus on memoir. Students will examine a variety of nonfiction writing that includes memoirs, biographies, autobiographies, and informational texts. The overarching goal is to increase reading comprehension through comparison and analysis of nonfiction elements and defining characteristics. Additionally, students will expand their writing skills by aligning their understanding of nonfiction writing with fiction and short story writing. By critically reading memoirs within the context of creative nonfiction, students will take on a reflective role as a reader and writer in order to conduct an in-depth analysis of memoir.

Using the metaphor of a photographer, students will learn how to focus their interest on a particular place, person, event, and memory in order to construct a personal memoir. Students will learn that, in contrast to biographical and autobiographical writing, a *memoir* is how one remembers one's own life or some part of one's life. An autobiography is history, requiring research, specific dates, and careful documentation. An autobiography traces a person's life from birth to some particular juncture in time, but a memoir usually narrows the lens. A memoir focuses on a particular time or series of events in the writer's

DOI: 10.4324/9781003235194-6

life that was unusually meaningful, such as childhood or adolescence, or that was framed by a personal, political, or newsworthy event, such as war, travel, or public service. Students will be encouraged to "focus" on a particular memory, and will explore how to closely examine, extend, and reflect on this event or time period through the use of colorful language, dialogue, and sensory details. Students will learn to "frame" their topic and examine the ways in which multiple perspectives influence the interpretation of a particular event, even altering the underlying message of a text. Finally, students will experience how their personal backgrounds, experiences, memories, and life events can provide an arsenal of creative devices for writing and sharing their personal stories with others.

More broadly, the activities and assessment products included in this unit are designed to help students develop a deeper understanding of the nonfiction genre and how it compares to fiction. Students should complete this unit with an understanding of different types of nonfiction writing and should be able to identify the characteristic story devices of memoir writing and the elements of style it shares with fiction and nonfiction. Students will have the opportunity to work with materials and ideas that suit their individual interests and need for challenge. At the completion of the unit, students will have completed a writing workshop aimed at guiding them through the writing process, including prewriting, drafting, editing, revising, and publishing a personal memoir. Their memoirs will be peer reviewed, then compiled into a class anthology. Excerpts of students' memoirs will be presented to an audience of students, parents, and teachers during the culminating Memoir Museum.

OBJECTIVES/STANDARDS

This unit is designed to be consistent with common state fourth-grade reading and writing standards, and national standards outlined by the National Council of Teachers of English (NCTE; National Council of Teachers of English & International Reading Association, 2012). It also aligns to the fourth-grade Common Core State Standards (CCSS; an alignment chart is provided on p. 259). This unit addresses the following objectives:

STUDENTS WILL KNOW THE FOLLOWING TERMS

- *Fiction* refers to stories that are not true.
- *Nonfiction* refers to stories that are factual or true.
- *Informational text* provides facts or information.
- *Biography* is when an outside person is telling us about another person's life.
- *Autobiography* is when a person is telling us about his or her own life.

- *Memoir* is a type of autobiography that is more personal and focuses on a memory and emotions rather than facts.
- *Perspective* involves interpreting an event from a different viewpoint.
- *Bias* involves emotions or opinions that can influence how material is presented.
- *Third-person point of view* is when the author tells a story about someone or something, using pronouns like *he* or *she.*
- *First-person point of view* is when the author tells a story about himself or herself, using pronouns like *me* or *I.*
- *Lens* is a narrow focus in which a story is viewed or told.
- *Genre* refers to a variety of different types of writing, distinguishable by specific characteristics.
- *Timeline* is a look at the major events of a person's life from birth to death.
- *Historical* stories tell about real-life events or history.
- *Chronological order* is when events are arranged from the earliest to the latest.
- *Sequence* is when events are put into the order in which they occurred.
- *Memory* is a formative event, time period, or relationship that an individual recalls with clarity.
- *Memoirist* is an individual who tells or writes memoirs.
- *Figurative language* is language the author uses to make a story more compelling.
- *Metaphor* is a figurative comparison of two different objects or ideas.
- *Simile* is a figurative comparison of two different objects or ideas using the words "like" or "as."
- *Supporting details* make a story stronger by adding more information, description, and background.
- *Emotional journey* refers to the gradual changes a character undergoes throughout a story as a response to a memorable event.
- *Sensory details* are descriptions that engage the senses.
- *Adjectives* are colorful words that add vivid description to writing.
- *Images* help the reader mentally visualize what is occurring in a text.
- To *reflect* means to take a closer look at yourself.
- *Frame* refers to the way an author presents a story in order to achieve the desired response from the reader.
- *External events* involve all of the actions that occur outside of the character.
- *Internal events* involve the thoughts and emotions that occur within the character.
- *Textual evidence* is written proof from a text that can be used to support an argument or claim.

- *Inference* is an understanding derived from implied rather than direct statements from the author.
- *Character traits* are words that describe a character's personality.
- *Author's purpose* is the writer's reason for writing: to inform, entertain, or persuade.
- *Theme* is the overarching message or lesson learned from a text.
- *Connections* occur when the reader shares an experience with the character.
- *Text-to-self connection* is when a student makes a connection between the text and his or her own real-world experiences.
- *Dialogue* refers to spoken (external) and unspoken (internal) speech or conversation that occurs between characters and is marked with quotations.
- *Internal dialogue* is unspoken conversation that occurs within a character's mind.
- *External dialogue* is spoken conversation that occurs between characters.
- *Prewriting* is when the author organizes his or her thoughts onto the paper prior to writing the first draft of the story.
- *First draft* is the initial, written version of the author's story.
- *Revising* is when the author improves his or her writing by examining language, sentence, and story choices.
- *Editing* is when the author improves his or her writing by checking for mechanical errors (spelling, grammar, punctuation) within the story.
- *Final draft* is the completed story that has been carefully revised and edited and is ready for publication.
- *Cover* is the front of a published text that contains the name of the story and author and is typically visually appealing.
- *Title page* is part of the front matter of a published text that appears between the cover and beginning of the text and restates the title and author.
- *Dedication* is one of the front matter pages of a published text in which the author gives a brief acknowledgement to another individual who positively influenced his or her story or writing.
- *Peer review* is when a writing is edited by one or more of the author's peers in order to gain constructive feedback, comments, or suggestions for revisions to improve the story.

STUDENTS WILL UNDERSTAND THE FOLLOWING BIG IDEAS ABOUT NONFICTION AND MEMOIR

- Perspective and purpose affect how we write and how we read the work of others.
- Experience shapes identity.

- Unique points of view are shaped by unique life experiences.
- We understand ourselves better when we work to make sense of our own experiences and the experiences of others.

STUDENTS WILL DEMONSTRATE THE FOLLOWING SKILLS

- Differentiate between fiction and nonfiction writing by exploring characteristics of each.
- Distinguish between the different nonfiction genres: biography, autobiography, memoir, and informational text.
- Explore how to tell a story through different lenses and multiple perspectives.
- Explore different examples of informational texts.
- Differentiate between different types of informational text.
- Apply knowledge of point of view and perspective to different types of nonfiction.
- Distinguish between the nonfiction genres of informational text and biography.
- Describe characteristics of a biography.
- Be able to tell a story through different lenses and multiple perspectives.
- Develop skills in looking for details that reflect moments in their lives.
- Define and describe the characteristics of autobiography.
- Compare and contrast biography and autobiography.
- Explore and describe memoir.
- Analyze memoirs for elements of story.
- Write about a meaningful memory (time period) or relationship.
- Use memoirs to closely examine the details of an event or time period in one's life.
- Identify the emotional journey presented in a memoir.
- Use compelling language when writing a memoir.
- Analyze memoirs for evidence or clues as to the author's character and purpose for writing.
- Understand the concept of using sensory language to create powerful writing.
- Identify the importance of framing a story.
- Use dialogue to enhance writing.
- Evaluate the quality of a memoir using specific characteristics of that genre.
- Write interesting story beginnings and endings.
- Draft, revise, edit, and publish a memoir.
- Present a well-written memoir to an audience using articulate presentation skills.

UNIT OUTLINE

	Big Idea(s)	Overview	Skills
Unit Preassessment			
Lesson 1	➢ Perspective and purpose affect how we write and how we read the work of others.	*Introduction to Nonfiction* ➢ Discuss differences between fiction and nonfiction. ➢ Discuss the differences between types of nonfiction.	➢ Differentiate between fiction and nonfiction writing by exploring characteristics of each. ➢ Distinguish between the different nonfiction genres: biography, autobiography, memoir, and informational text.
Lesson 2	➢ Perspective and purpose affect how we write and how we read the work of others.	*Looking Through the Lens* ➢ Explore a variety of nonfiction texts that present an event using multiple perspectives.	➢ Explore how to tell a story through different lenses and multiple perspectives. ➢ Explore different examples of informational texts.
Formative Assessment 1			
Lesson 3	➢ Perspective and purpose affect how we write and how we read the work of others.	*Get Informed* ➢ Explore informational texts.	➢ Differentiate between different types of informational text. ➢ Apply knowledge of point of view and perspective to different types of nonfiction.
Lesson 4	➢ Perspective and purpose affect how we write and how we read the work of others. ➢ Experience shapes identity.	*Biography: Sequencing Versus a Single Event* ➢ Explore the biography genre. ➢ Differentiate between a sequence of events vs. a single event.	➢ Distinguish between the nonfiction genres informational text and biography. ➢ Describe characteristics of biography. ➢ Be able to tell a story through different lenses and multiple perspectives.
Lesson 5	➢ Perspective and purpose affect how we write and how we read the work of others. ➢ Experience shapes identity. ➢ Unique points of view are shaped by unique life experiences.	*Autobiography: Interviewing an Expert* ➢ Writing autobiographies and biographies.	➢ Develop skills in looking for details that reflect moments in their lives. ➢ Define and describe the characteristics of autobiography ➢ Compare and contrast biography and autobiography.
Lesson 6	➢ Perspective and purpose affect how we write and how we read the work of others. ➢ Experience shapes identity. ➢ Unique points of view are shaped by unique life experiences.	*Introduction to Memoir* ➢ Introduce memoir.	➢ Develop skills in looking for details that reflect moments in their lives. ➢ Explore and describe memoir.

	Big Idea(s)	Overview	Skills
Formative Assessment 2			
Lesson 7	➢ Perspective and purpose affect how we write and how we read the work of others. ➢ We understand ourselves better when we work to make sense of our own experiences and the experiences of others.	*Focusing on a Memory, Event, or Relationship* ➢ Brainstorm ideas for a personal memoir.	➢ Analyze memoirs for elements of story. ➢ Write about a meaningful memory, event (time period), or relationship.
Lesson 8	➢ Perspective and purpose affect how we write and how we read other's work.	*Examining an Event* ➢ Identify how a writer can expand a single moment into an emotional journey.	➢ Use memoirs to closely examine the details of an event or time period in one's life. ➢ Identify the emotional journey presented in a memoir.
Lesson 9	➢ Perspective and purpose affect how we write and how we read the work of others. ➢ Experience shapes identity. ➢ We understand ourselves better when we work to make sense of our own experiences and the experiences of others.	*Showing, Not Telling* ➢ Practice using sensory details.	➢ Use compelling language when writing a memoir. ➢ Analyze memoirs for evidence or clues as to the author's character and purpose for writing. ➢ Students will understand the concept of using sensory language to create powerful writing.
Formative Assessment 3 + Optional Formative Assessment			
Lesson 10	➢ Perspective and purpose affect how we write and how we read the work of others. ➢ Experience shapes identity. ➢ We understand ourselves better when we work to make sense of our own experiences and the experiences of others.	*Framing Your Topic* ➢ Strategies for taking notes and monitoring reading comprehension using nonfiction texts.	➢ Distinguish between different nonfiction genres: biography, autobiography, memoir, and informational text. ➢ Identify the importance of framing a story.
Lesson 11	➢ Perspective and purpose affect how we write and how we read the work of others. ➢ Experience shapes identity. ➢ We understand ourselves better when we work to make sense of our own experiences and the experiences of others.	*What's the Point?* ➢ Explore memoir writing to identify the speaker and purpose. ➢ Use textual evidence to support opinions.	➢ Analyze memoirs for evidence or clues as to the author's character and purpose for writing. ➢ Identify the emotional journey presented in a memoir.

	Big Idea(s)	Overview	Skills
Lesson 12	⪢ We understand ourselves better when we work to make sense of our own experiences and the experiences of others.	*Author's Craft* ⪢ Write about a meaningful memory, event (time period) or relationship. ⪢ Utilize internal and external dialogue.	⪢ Write about a meaningful memory, event (time period) or relationship. ⪢ Use dialogue to enhance their writing.
Formative Assessment 4			
Lesson 13	⪢ Perspective and purpose affect how we write and how we read the work of others. ⪢ We understand ourselves better when we work to make sense of our own experiences and the experiences of others.	*Writing Workshop: Prewriting and First Drafts* ⪢ Craft strong beginnings and endings for memoirs.	⪢ Write interesting story beginnings and endings. ⪢ Draft, revise, edit, and publish a memoir.
Lesson 14	⪢ Perspective and purpose affect how we write and how we read the work of others. ⪢ Experience shapes identity. ⪢ We understand ourselves better when we work to make sense of our own experiences and the experiences of others. ⪢ Unique points of view are shaped by unique life experiences.	*Writing Workshop: Revising and Editing* ⪢ Drafting, revision, and writing.	⪢ Identify the importance of revising and editing their work. ⪢ Draft, revise, edit, and publish a memoir.
Lesson 15	⪢ Perspective and purpose affect how we write and how we read the work of others. ⪢ We understand ourselves better when we work to make sense of our own experiences and the experiences of others.	*Writing Workshop: Peer Review and Final Drafts* ⪢ Peer review and write final drafts.	⪢ Write interesting story beginnings and endings. ⪢ Draft, revise, edit, and publish a memoir.
Lesson 16	⪢ Perspective and purpose affect how we write and how we read the work of others. ⪢ We understand ourselves better when we work to make sense of our own experiences and the experiences of others.	*Memoir Museum* ⪢ Present memoirs to peers, parents, and other visitors at a Memoir Museum.	⪢ Present their memoir to an audience.
Lesson 17: Performance Task (Summative Assessment)			

PREPARING TO TEACH THE UNIT

RESOURCES AND MATERIALS

Throughout the unit, the teacher will read a variety of narratives that provide a representative sample of memoir writing. These texts are written well above student reading levels, but contain sophisticated themes and messages conducive for close analysis, which predisposes them to thoughtful discussion. Additionally, each story provides an exemplar for the lesson's focus. Links to web-based lesson materials are provided in each lesson plan and on the book's webpage at https://www.routledge.com/9781618216496.

CLASSROOM ENVIRONMENT

The teacher is encouraged to set up a classroom environment that is conducive to whole-class read alouds, group collaboration, and independent work. Establishing a daily routine and a consistent classroom physical environment is imperative. Here are some very practical tips to help you execute a successful unit:

- Help students set up and organize journals; they will glue a ribbon in the back of to serve as a bookmark. The ribbon will indicate when the student wants the teacher to view his or her personal writing.
- Identify a prominent place in the classroom for a word wall, where important vocabulary and terms can be prominently displayed throughout the unit.

CLASSROOM MANAGEMENT

The writing workshop portion of this unit will rely heavily on the classroom management of the teacher. During this time, the teacher will monitor the progress of the class as a whole, while also regulating and monitoring the learning progress of writers at varying levels of sophistication and writing expertise. The following are suggestions for classroom management during the writing workshop (see Lesson 13):

- Prominently display the steps of the writing process that students will move through. Encourage students to monitor their own progress through self-regulated learning by moving their clothespin to the writing stage where they are currently working.
- Designate areas of the room for independent writing, teacher conferences, and collaboration, with writing materials organized for easy accessibility.

ONGOING ASSESSMENT

The unit preassessment is administered to students prior to the first lesson. The purpose of the preassessment is (1) to assess what students already know about the purpose and structure of nonfiction texts as well as effective research strategies, which will help tailor the activities and group students appropriately, and (2) to provide a baseline for comparison at the end of the unit so that the teacher can assess the growth of each student throughout the course of the unit.

Formative assessments are administered to students throughout the unit in order to (1) assess students' developing skills so that resources and activities can be tailored to each student, and (2) assess what students already know about research, which will help tailor the activities and group students appropriately.

There are two summative assessments for this unit. The first is the culminating project ending in the Memoir Museum. Students' final products will serve as the evidence of their learning and the provided rubric will serve as the evaluation tool. There will also be a performance task conducted the day after the Memoir Museum. All of the necessary materials are provided for this assignment.

THE CLEAR CURRICULUM MODEL

This unit has been designed using the CLEAR Curriculum Model. The CLEAR (Challenge Leading to Engagement, Achievement and Results) Curriculum incorporates elements from three research-based curriculum models—differentiation, depth and complexity, and the Schoolwide Enrichment Model—by Carol Tomlinson, Sandra Kaplan, and Joseph Renzulli, respectively. These elements are applied to a curriculum framework that is consistent with state and national standards in reading, but builds layers of challenge and opportunities for more in-depth study authentic to the work of professionals within a discipline, to better meet the needs of all students. Refer to p. 15 for more information about the CLEAR Curriculum Model.

ICONS EXPLAINED

Integrated throughout the lesson plans are a series of icons or symbols intended to draw your attention to the particular content focus, learning objective, or instructional configuration of each learning activity. Some of these icons are derived from Sandra Kaplan's Depth and Complexity curriculum model, while others have been developed specifically for the CLEAR Curriculum Model used in these units. Refer to p. 16 for an explanation of each icon.

LESSON 1 Introduction to Nonfiction

MATERIALS

- Video examples of nonfiction:
  - "Sally Ride—Mini Biography" (available at http://www.biography.com/people/sally-ride-9458284/videos/sally-ride-mini-biography-13042755781)
  - "Finding Your Roots With Henry Louis Gates Jr.: Prof. Gates' Story" (available at https://www.youtube.com/watch?v=gd5A_GFbaSc)
  - "Marley & Me Movie Trailer" (available at https://www.youtube.com/watch?v=0UMMGNxg1Lg)
  - "How to Juggle Three Balls" (available at https://www.youtube.com/watch?v=kCt1bmSASCI)
- Handout 1.1: Unit Preassessment

Perspective and purpose affect how we write and how we read the work of others.

OBJECTIVES

Students will:

- differentiate between fiction and nonfiction writing by exploring characteristics of each; and
- distinguish between the different nonfiction genres: biography, autobiography, memoir, and informational text.

- Fiction
- Nonfiction
- Informational text
- Biography
- Autobiography
- Memoir

SEQUENCE

UNIT PREASSESSMENT

1. Administer the Unit Preassessment (Handout 1.1). Explain to students that this assessment is not for a grade. Rather, it is to find out how much they already know about nonfiction.

WARM UP

Ensure students understand *fiction* and *nonfiction*. These words are likely familiar to fourth graders, but a mini-lesson may be necessary.

2. Tell students that, in this unit, they will read and analyze a variety of *nonfiction*. This word has the prefix *non-*. Ask students to think of other words that have this prefix (*nonexistent, nonessential, nonconformist,* etc.) What does the prefix *non-* mean? (Not.) Therefore, *nonfiction* refers to stories that are "not *fiction*." *Fiction*, on the other hand, involves stories that are made up. Then, ask students to define *fiction*. Add *fiction* and *nonfiction* to the word wall (see p. 145).

ACTIVITY: OVERVIEW OF NONFICTION

3. Explain to students that they will watch several video clips to help introduce them to four types of nonfiction writing. You will *not* tell them what type of nonfiction the video is before they watch it. They will watch each clip, then discuss what type of nonfiction it is and explain the definition.
4. Have students watch the Sally Ride video.

As students watch, review their preassessments. Create one pile for any students who named/defined *biography*, *autobiography*, *memoir*, and some type of informational text, and a pile for students who identified only one or two genres. Use this data to call on students who are more familiar with types of nonfiction so that they can provide the answers for their peers.

5. Ask students to name the type of nonfiction they just watched and to provide a definition. Provide the term *biography* if needed. If students do not know the definition, ask: *What kind of information are we getting from this clip?* (Information about Sally Ride/an astronaut.) *Is Sally Ride telling us about herself, or is it someone else?* (Someone else.) Explain that *biography* is when an outside person is telling us about a person's life. Display the definition.
6. Have students watch the Henry Louis Gates video. Ask students to name the type of nonfiction they just watched and provide a definition. Provide the term *autobiography* if needed. If students do not know the

definition, ask: *What kind of information are we getting from this clip?* (Information about Henry Louis Gates.) *Is Henry Louis Gates telling us about himself, or is it someone else?* (He is talking about himself.) Explain that *auto-* means "self," so an *autobiography* is when a person is telling us about his or her life. Display the definition.

7. Have students watch the *Marley & Me* trailer. Ask students to name the type of nonfiction they just watched and provide a definition. Provide the term *memoir* if needed. If students do not know the definition, ask: *What kind of information are we getting from this clip?* (Information about a family and its dog.) *Who is telling us this information?* (The dog owner.) Ask if they think the clip is more like *biography* or *autobiography* (autobiography). Help students understand that *memoir* is a type of *autobiography* that is more personal because there is a narrow topic (the dog, not the owner's entire life) and it deals more with feelings than facts. Display the definition.
8. Have students watch the juggling how-to video. Ask students to name the type of nonfiction they just watched and provide a definition. Provide the term *informational text* if needed. Ask them what the video and these texts have in common (they are providing information). If students do not know any informational texts, ask them what they saw in the video (a person juggling) and help them understand that they were getting information about how to juggle. *Informational texts* provide facts or information. Display the definition.
9. Explain that, in the upcoming lessons, students will be looking at these different types of nonfiction in more depth. However, students will ultimately focus on *memoir*, which sometimes incorporates stylistic elements of fiction. Add *autobiography, biography, informational text*, and *memoir* to the word wall.

CLOSE

10. Take students to the library to see nonfiction texts. Invite the librarian to explain how the library is organized and where they can find the different types. As students explore the library, ask them to create lists of books they find that fit each nonfiction genre (autobiography, biography, informational text, memoir). Explain that they might have some overlap between autobiography and memoir, which is okay at this stage.

Keep a variety of nonfiction books in your classroom for students to reference. If you cannot go to the library, allow students to discuss the different types of books you have on hand.

HANDOUT 1.1

UNIT PREASSESSMENT

Directions: Answer the following questions about nonfiction texts.

1. List any examples of nonfiction books, movies, TV shows, etc., that you know.

2. Name, define, and give an example for as many genres of nonfiction as you can.

3. What is the difference between first-person and third-person point of view?

LESSON 2 Looking Through the Lens

MATERIALS

- Excerpts from *The Story of My Life* by Hellen Keller (available at http://www.gutenberg.org/files/2397/2397-h/2397-h.htm)
- Images to display:
  - "Different Focal Lengths" (available at http://blog.vidaao.com/wp-content/uploads/different-focal-lengths.png)
  - "Neutral Density Filtered" (available at http://digital-photography-school.com/wp-content/uploads/2008/02/diy-nd-filter.jpg)
  - "UV Ultraviolet" (available at https://images-na.ssl-images-amazon.com/images/I/5199J-9CP6L.jpg)
- Handout 2.1: Formative Assessment 1
- Appendix B1: Formative Assessment 1 Answer Key

Perspective and purpose affect how we write and how we read the work of others.

OBJECTIVES

Students will:

- explore how to tell a story through different lenses and multiple perspectives, and
- explore different examples of informational texts.

- Perspective
- Bias
- Third-person point of view
- First-person point of view
- Lens

SEQUENCE

WARM UP

1. Briefly review each type of nonfiction (autobiography, biography, informational text, and memoir) based on the lists students created at the library. If any students have wrong answers, work together as a class to categorize the work properly.

In the preassessment, students were asked to define first- and third-person point of view. If you have students who were unclear about these terms, plan a mini-lesson on point of view.

If students are more familiar with point of view, you can mention that some informational texts, such as instructional manuals, use second-person point of view. Show them a website like wikiHow (e.g., http://www.wikihow.com/Do-Well-in-School) so they can see that instructional manuals are often directly addressing the reader. Other informational texts, such as newspapers, typically use third person.

INSTRUCTION: POINT OF VIEW

2. Explain to students that they are going to take a closer look at nonfiction with two pieces about Helen Keller from her book *The Story of My Life*. Invite students to find a comfortable place to listen. Tell them that they will want to think about which type of nonfiction they are listening to.
3. Read aloud to students an excerpt from Section I, Chapter I ("I am told that while I was still in long dresses . . ." through "cried for her to take me up in her arms."). Ask students if they think it is autobiography, biography, informational text, or memoir. As necessary, help them understand that this passage represents *autobiography* because Helen Keller is talking about herself, recounting pivotal events from her life, but she is not talking about a specific memory or emotion, which would make it a memoir. Ask what point of view is used in autobiography and memoir. Students should understand that they use first person. The author is telling his or her own story, using pronouns like *I* and *me*.
4. Read aloud to students a second excerpt from Section III, Chapter II ("Mark Twain has said . . ." through "invented by the Abbe de l'Epee."). Ask students if they think it is autobiography, biography, informational text, or memoir. As necessary, help them understand that this passage represents *biography* because, in this section of the book, an outside person is telling the reader about Helen Keller. The writer is discussing a specific person, not just presenting information about a topic, which would make it informational text. Ask what point of view is used in biography and informational text. Students should understand that it is third person. The author is telling a story about someone or something, using pronouns like *he*, *she*, and *they*.
5. Add *first-person point of view* and *third-person point of view* to the word wall.

INSTRUCTION: PERSPECTIVE

6. Explain that to really understand nonfiction, students have to take perspective into account. Tell students: A person telling a story may tell a single event from a different perspective or may bring different perspec-

tives and experiences to an event, which can change the way an event is interpreted and the way a story is told.

7. Explain that it is like taking photograph. Photographers take pictures with a camera, and sometimes they change the lens or filter that they are looking through. The photographer can change the lens (http://blog.vidaao.com/wp-content/uploads/different-focal-lengths.png) to show either a lot about what is happening, or to focus it on something smaller. Show students how adding a filter (http://digital-photography-school.com/wp-content/uploads/2008/02/diy-nd-filter.jpg, or https://images-na.ssl-images-amazon.com/images/I/5199J-9CP6L.jpg) changes the way a picture looks, just how different emotions can change how an event looks to a person. Add *lens* to the word wall.
8. Say: When we let our emotions influence us, it often shows our bias, or our opinions, of the events. Which types of nonfiction are more likely to have our bias or opinions in it? Help students understand that the works written from a first-person point of view are more likely to have bias because there is often only one perspective of the events.
9. Add *bias* and *perspective* to the word wall.

ACTIVITY: PERSPECTIVE TAKING

10. Instruct students to fold a sheet paper of paper into three sections. Tell students to think of an important event in their life so far that they are comfortable sharing with a partner.
    - ✓ In the top section, students should write a one-paragraph memory from the perspective of a friend or family member.
    - ✓ In the middle section, they should write a paragraph about the event from their own perspective.
    - ✓ And, in the bottom section, they should write a paragraph from the perspective of someone who does not know them at all.

If students struggle to engage in this form of perspective taking, try to identify a controversial character in a story students may be familiar with. For example, you might ask them to first discuss how an event in the story of Little Red Riding Hood would be different from the wolf's perspective or the grandmother's perspective.

Encourage students to fully embrace each role they take on, but remind them that each paragraph must cover the same event. As they write, they should keep in mind how the different perspectives and biases change the way they portray the event.

2E

For some students with challenges in written expression or who struggle to write paragraphs quickly without assistance, consider offering an option for students to have a scribe or to engage in this activity orally.

11. Allow students to share their paragraphs (either as a class or in small groups, depending on the number of students you have). As a class, discuss the following questions: *How does writing from a different perspective change how you view an event? How does your perspective affect how you understand other events?* Help students understand that everyone has feelings and opinions about events. These shape our individual perspectives, and play a role in how we write and how we feel about what we read.

PREPARATION: FORMATIVE ASSESSMENT 1

12. Administer Formative Assessment 1 (Handout 2.1). An answer key is provided (Appendix B1).
13. **Using the assessment data:** Separate students into three groups for a writing activity in the next lesson.
    - ✓ **Group A:** Students have difficulty with writing and/or are weaker in identifying different perspectives and bias within the text.
    - ✓ **Group B:** Students are stronger writers and/or seem to understand well but need a little more guidance.
    - ✓ **Group C:** Students are the strongest writers and consistently (and correctly) work with the ideas presented.

HANDOUT 2.1

FORMATIVE ASSESSMENT 1

Directions: Answer the following questions with what you know about bias, perspective, and point of view.

1. Read the following two paragraphs about the 2016 Olympic games.

Paragraph 1:

During the 2016 Olympic games in Rio de Janeiro, South Korea's Kim Woo-jin set a world record in Olympic archery. The world champion's total of 700 points during the competition eclipsed the previous record of 699 set by another Korean, Im Dong-hyun, at the London Olympics 4 years ago. Although he dazzled his Olympic rivals and thrilled the small crowd in the terraces, the poker-faced Kim played down his achievement.

Paragraph 2:

During the 2012 and 2016 Olympic games, the very superior Korean archers, who have the best training in the world, earned well-deserved accolades for their untouchable prowess. They outshone their competitors by setting new world records. It was surprising that Kim Woo-jin could achieve this record despite the poor judges at this event.

a. Which of these paragraphs is more biased?

b. Indicate the words and phrases that indicate bias in the paragraph you identified as more biased.

Note. Paragraphs 1 and 2 are adapted from Ransom, 2016.

HANDOUT 2.1, CONTINUED

2. Read these two descriptions about Carolyn.

Description 1:

Carolyn was always a studious girl who followed the rules, but she didn't submit the required essay for the competition. Why was she being so stubborn about this assignment? She knew she will get a failing grade and it will affect the grade she gets on her report card so she should have just done it!

Description 2:

How can they ask me to write about things I don't believe in? They can't make me do it and I will just take the failing grade. And I don't think we should be competing in our writing anyway. We should just all do the best we can.

a. Which of these descriptions is told in first-person point of view?

b. What are the differences between first-person point of view and third-person point of view?

LESSON

3 Get Informed

MATERIALS

- ✓ Student journals
- ✓ Variety of informational texts
- ✓ Variety of craft supplies (pipe cleaners, cotton balls, paper, etc.)

Perspective and purpose affect how we write and how we read the work of others.

OBJECTIVES

Students will:

- ✓ differentiate between different types of informational text, and
- ✓ apply knowledge of point of view and perspective to different types of nonfiction.

SEQUENCE

WARM UP

1. Divide students into small, mixed-ability groups based on the results of the preassessment (students who were able to identify and define types of informational text working with students who were not able to do so). Ask them to complete a scavenger hunt for different types of informational texts, writing down the title of the text and what type of text they think it is.
2. Give students 5–10 minutes to complete this search, and then ask them to share the different types and titles. Compile a list of students' findings on the board. Discuss why students might have made any mistakes and correct their misconceptions.

You likely have a lot of informational texts in the room—textbooks, dictionaries, rules, etc. Consider bringing in additional texts to supplement what you usually have, such as instruction manuals or food items (with nutritional facts).

3. Ask: *What do all these informational texts have in common?* Make sure students are connecting with the ideas discussed during the lesson on point of view (largely third person, though they may come across some second person) and perspective (focused on the matter it means to inform, reporting facts without bias/emotional attachment).

Allow students to decorate their journals with pictures, drawings, and other decorations to make journals their own. This will ensure that students take ownership of their work and make the writing process more personal.

ACTIVITY: WRITING INFORMATIONAL TEXT

4. Refer students to their journals (see p. 145). Explain that throughout the unit their journals will be used for class notes, journal responses, and written accounts of personal experiences and memories. Students can bookmark pages with a ribbon that they want to share with others, or fold down the corner of a page to keep it private.
5. Divide students into the groups determined by Formative Assessment 1.
   - ✓ **Group A** will write an informational paragraph about point of view and perspective in informational text.
   - ✓ **Group B** will write an informational paragraph about a topic of their choice, using third-person point of view and an unbiased, outside perspective.
   - ✓ **Group C** will write an informational paragraph about how point of view and perspective can change depending on the type of nonfiction.

6. Give students about 5–10 minutes to complete the activity. Afterward, divide them into new groups, so that each new group has at least one student from Group 1, one student from Group 2, and one student from Group 3. Have group members share their paragraphs with each other, starting with students originally in Group 1. Encourage them to use the information they get from each other to improve their writing (e.g., noting any instances where emotion comes in, using the wrong pronouns).

Review the paragraphs of any early finishers and challenge them to edit their writing by noting any instances where they can add more clarity or detail. Then, allow them to explore the informational texts in the room or free write in their journals about their thoughts and feelings about the unit so far.

7. Afterward, have students find a partner. Explain that they are going to create a set of directions for their partner to follow. The goal will be for students to write the directions so clearly that their partner will create the exact same thing. Depending on resources available, you can have students simply draw a picture or construct an object out of materials

like pipe cleaners, cotton balls, paper, etc. Just make sure that students know to get double the supplies so their partner will have everything he or she needs.

8. Give students 3–5 minutes to create their drawing, object, etc. Then, give them an additional 5 minutes to write the directions for their partner to create the object. Make sure they know that they cannot talk to their partner, and that they need to make sure their partner cannot see what they are drawing/creating.
9. After time is up, tell students to give the directions and any necessary materials to their partners. Remind them that they are not allowed to talk during the activity. Give them about 5 minutes to draw/create based on their partner's instructions, then have them compare their works.
10. Ask: *How many of you did not draw/create the same object? What were the directions missing?* (Common issues: They were told to make shapes/folds but were not given a size/length, the directions used imprecise words [e.g., about, kind of, sort of], there was no clear focus/title so the partner did not even know what he or she should aim for.) *What does this tell us about informational text?* (Focus and clear/precise directions are important.)
11. Ask: *How many of you drew/created the exact same object? What did the directions say that helped you the most? What could have been changed or added to make the directions more clear?* Students should understand that clear, concise directions—that present the facts needed and nothing else—are easier to follow.
12. Explain to students that, as they work through nonfiction, that the goal will always be to write clearly so that the reader understands the writer's purpose and perspective. Because the reader will not be able to see things exactly from the author's point of view, making the author's perspective clear, even in informational text, is crucial.

Although it is okay for students write down directions while they craft their creation, the time guidelines are meant to put the focus on actually writing directions.

LESSON 4 Biography: Sequencing Versus a Single Event

MATERIALS

- Student computer and Internet access to selected biography sources:
  - **Group A:** "Biographies for Kids: Famous Leaders for Young Readers" by Garden of Praise (available at http://gardenofpraise.com/leaders.htm)
  - **Group B:** "Biography—For Kids: Life Stories" by Ducksters (available at http://www.ducksters.com/biography)
  - **Group C:** "Biographies for Kids" by TurtleDiary.com (available at https://www.turtlediary.com/biographies.html)
- Sentence strips
- Sticky notes
- Handout 4.1: Biography Facts

- Perspective and purpose affect how we write and how we read the work of others.
- Experience shapes identity.

OBJECTIVES

Students will:

- distinguish between the nonfiction genres of informational text and biography,
- describe characteristics of a biography, and
- be able to tell a story through different lenses and multiple perspectives.

- Genre
- Timeline
- Historical
- Chronological Order
- Sequence

SEQUENCE

WARM UP

1. Students will continue to explore and identify different genres of nonfiction. Ask students to review genres of nonfiction other than informational text. Discuss until they identify *biography*.
2. Ask students if they are familiar with the word *timeline* and what the purpose of one is. Students should understand that, in a biography or autobiography, a timeline is a look at the major events of a person's life from birth to death (or some significant point in a person's life). The timeline usually starts from the earliest event told to the latest. Add *timeline* to the word wall.

ACTIVITY: READING EXAMPLES OF NONFICTION

3. Divide students into pairs within the following groups based on readiness determined by Formative Assessment 1 results, focusing specifically on their performance on the questions assessing reading comprehension.
   - ✓ **Group A:** Students who demonstrated a strong understanding of the passages from Formative Assessment 1 will visit Garden of Praise, which includes lengthy biographies with real artifacts and sophisticated language.
   - ✓ **Group B:** Students who demonstrated a moderate understanding of the passages will visit Ducksters, which includes shorter biographies organized into sections.
   - ✓ **Group C:** Students who demonstrated limited or no understanding of the passages should visit TurtleDiary.com, which includes shorter biographies with keywords underlined and explained, illustrations, etc.

4. Distribute Handout 4.1: Biography Facts and sentence strips. With their partners, ask students to (1) select a biography of interest, (2) read the biography together, (3) complete the handout, and (4) create a timeline for their individual on the sentence strip.

Early finishers should select three events from the biography they read. They should be events they believe would likely be the most memorable to the person and would evoke strong feelings. They should justify the reasons for their selections and write an explanation for how each event could be important enough to be the subject of a memoir.

DISCUSSION: CHARACTERISTICS OF BIOGRAPHY

5. Display the word *biography*. Ask students to think about the biographies they read and to consider what they learned: *What kind of information do you get from a biography? What characteristics does a biography have?*
6. Distribute several sticky notes to each student. Ask students to share characteristics they think a story needs in order to be a biography and record one characteristic on each sticky note. (Critical responses: It's about a person's life, it's about history, it tells facts, it's told in third person, it's supposed to be unbiased, it's based on careful documentation of events, etc.) Encourage students to write as many sticky notes as they can.
7. One at a time, have students share their sticky notes with the class. Encourage them to share new ideas. If a student does not have a new idea, go to the next student. As they share, ask students to display their sticky notes under the word *biography*. Have them decide how to cluster similar responses into groups.
8. Once all notes have been shared, work as a class to make a master list of the characteristics of biography. One characteristic should be that biographies are historical, or tell about real-life events.
9. Examine the word *autobiography*. Break this word into *auto* and *biography*. Ask students to name other words beginning with *auto* (e.g., *automatic, automobile, autograph*). The root *auto* means "self." Students will be examining the autobiography genre in the next lesson.
10. Tell students that in fiction, stories are often—but not always—organized into a beginning, middle, and end. Ask: *How were the biographies you read organized? Did they follow a specific structure? How were the events ordered? How do the events relate to what you learned about timelines?* Students should understand that most biographies are written in chronological order and in a sequence from the earliest event to the latest event. Use a sentence strip to show students how a timeline flows from the left hand side to the right. Add *chronological order* and *sequence* to the word wall.

ACTIVITY: CREATING A PERSONAL TIMELINE

11. Encourage students to pause and think about their lives. Ask: *What are the high points of your life so far (e.g., being given an award, getting a new pet, having a new sibling)? What are low points of your life so far (e.g., death of a family member, moving to a new town, struggling in a school subject, etc.)?* Ask students why a high point in one person's life could be a low point in someone else's life (e.g., when one student is chosen to be a lead in a play, someone else did not get the part).

Explain that nonfiction can involve very personal writing experiences. Students will be exploring past experiences, feelings, and emotions. Encourage students to be open and honest because this will help ensure that their writing is rich and compelling, but they should never feel like they need to write about topics that they feel are too personal or painful. They should also be very respectful of others' work.

12. Distribute sentence strips. Ask students to create a timeline of their lives, sequencing the major events of their life from birth to present. Encourage students to include as many big events as possible, but not every event. Some students may need more than one sentence strip.
13. Afterward, ask them to look closely at their timelines: *Which events were low points? High points? How have these events led you to where you are or what you value today?*
14. Reiterate that biographies describe all or most of the important, historical events of another person's life (or a period of that person's life) in sequential order. Emphasize that biographies are supposed to be unbiased, meaning that they should simply tell and analyze the facts, or information about what happened. No emotion, opinions, or feelings of the author should be associated with the biography unless backed up with actual facts.

Students have usually been asked to write about themselves with a more biographical/fact-oriented perspective, so this may be more difficult and uncomfortable for them. Consider sharing an example from your own life to model the difference between just telling about an event and telling how an event influenced you or illustrated a powerful feeling you have.

ACTIVITY: FINDING A MOMENT IN TIME

15. Ask students to look at their timelines: *Is there a story in one of these points in your timeline that results from a single high or low moment in your life? Does one of the high points or low points show how you have grown or changed or learned a lesson? Does one of the high or low points illustrate how you feel very strongly about something or reflect the kind of person you are? The high or low point can be about your family, school, or life or how you experienced something happening in history* (choose a recent historical event that students have discussed).
16. Have students add their timelines to their journals. On the next page, ask students to write down a title for a memorable event they want to explore further. Have students write about that topic, thinking back on the feelings, emotions, and memories. If students want you to review their writing, remind them they can bookmark the page.

2E

- Emphasize that sentences and punctuation are not important during this time; the main goal is for students to begin reflecting about their important life experiences and to begin putting their thoughts on paper.
- If you have students who struggle with written expression, consider scribing for them, allowing them to draw their memory in detail, or providing assistive technology to them.

HOMEWORK: WALK THE NEIGHBORHOOD

17. For homework, ask students to take a walk around their neighborhood, or to simply look out the window where they live, and view the street and surrounding area. Tell them to think about what they see, small, taste, hear, and touch. Ask students to form a mental image of their

neighborhood or their view from the window. They will use the mental image in the next lesson, so they should try to focus on and recall as many details as possible. They can make notes or draw a picture if they wish.

Name: ______________________ **Date:** ____________

HANDOUT 4.1

BIOGRAPHY FACTS

Directions: Visit your assigned website and pick a biographical sketch that interests you. Read the biographical sketch and answer the questions about the person below.

1. Full name:
2. Age (if still alive):
3. Year of birth:
4. Where did he or she live?
5. Cause and year of death (if not still alive):
6. What was his or her family like? Was he or she married? Did he or she have children?
7. Why is he or she important or famous?
8. What is he or she best remembered for?

HANDOUT 4.1, CONTINUED

9. Name three of the most important events in his or her life:

10. Share at least one fun fact that you learned about this person:

Now, use a sentence strip to make a timeline for your person. Remember to start with the earliest dates and go to the last. Only include the most important events! Staple your timeline to this sheet. You may need more than one sentence strip.

LESSON

5 Autobiography: Interviewing an Expert

MATERIALS

- ✓ White paper (one per student)
- ✓ Excerpt from Mark Twain's Autobiography (available at http://gutenberg.net.au/ebooks02/0200551h.html)
- ✓ Handout 5.1: Interview an Expert
- ✓ Handout 5.2: Biography Versus Autobiography
- ✓ Appendix B2: Biography Versus Autobiography Answer Key

- Perspective and purpose affect how we write and how we read the work of others.
- Experience shapes identity.
- Unique points of view are shaped by unique life experiences.

OBJECTIVES

Students will:

- ✓ develop skills in looking for details that reflect moments in their lives,
- ✓ define and describe the characteristics of autobiography, and
- ✓ compare and contrast biography and autobiography.

SEQUENCE

WARM UP

1. Remind students of their homework. Ask students to close their eyes and picture their neighborhood, street, or house/apartment: *What does this setting look like? What kinds of things do you see, hear, smell, touch, and taste? How would you describe where you live to someone who has never been there?*

2. Have students work with their shoulder partners. Partners will take turns describing their neighborhood, street, house, etc., while the other draws what he or she hears. After each student finishes drawing, partners should determine how accurate it is and discuss what additional details would have been useful to hear to make it more accurate.
3. Afterward, ask:
   - ✓ What important lessons did you learn from this activity? What did you learn about writing—or speaking—with compelling language and sensory detail?
   - ✓ What role did perspective play in this activity?
   - ✓ Have you ever felt so familiar with something that you feel too close to it to describe it clearly? What important insight does this provide us about the process of writing an autobiography?

4. Have students look at the drawing of their neighborhood, house, or apartment. They can also identify another place they have a strong connection with. Explain that memoirists often while about places that hold poignant memories. Allow students time to reflect and briefly write about any memories, good or bad, they associate with the place that they choose.

READ ALOUD

5. Read aloud an excerpt from the autobiography of Mark Twain, Volume I, "Early Years in Florida, Missouri" (para. 1–3, ""I was born the 30th of November . . ." through "the church was a schoolhouse.").
6. Ask: *Based on the details the writer provides, what images of this neighborhood come to mind? What emotions would you feel if you visited this neighborhood? Who lives there?* Then, ask students to consider: *Are there people who would feel uncomfortable in your neighborhood? Do people judge you or make assumptions about your character because of where you live? How was this reflected in Mark Twain's autobiography?*

INSTRUCTION: BIOGRAPHY VERSUS AUTOBIOGRAPHY

7. Discuss the differences between biography and autobiography. Remind students that autobiography has an added prefix. Therefore, both genres are the same except for one main, important difference. Encourage students to use what they remember know about words that share the prefix *auto-* (e.g., *autograph, autoimmune, automobile, automatic*) to reiterate the difference between a biography and an autobiography.

Use a Venn diagram to review. Although both genres are sequential and historical retellings of a person's life, another person writes a biography, while the actual person the story is about writes an autobiography. Be sure students remember that that *auto-* is a Greek prefix that means "self;" therefore, *autobiography* literally means "self-biography," or a biography written by the self.

ACTIVITY: INTERVIEWING AN EXPERT

8. Ask: *Who is a better expert on who you are than you?* Tell students that to further explore their lives, they will be interviewed about their life, and they will interview a friend about his or her life. Allow students to select partners.
9. Distribute Handout 5.1: Interview an Expert. Ask students to use the timelines they created in Lesson 4. Give students time to exchange timelines and interview each other. Encourage students to be thoughtful and creative in their answers, digging deeper than surface level details and facts. Remind students to think about things they saw, felt, heard, smelled, etc., at these times.

Some students might have difficulty "digging deep" in this exercise. Consider modeling an interview for students. Consider showing a brief video clip (e.g., "Katie Couric on how to conduct a good interview," available at https://www.youtube.com/watch?v=4eOynrI2eTM).

- **Writing a biography:** After the interviews, have students use their handouts and their partner's timelines to write paragraph-long biographies about their classmates. Remind students that biographies are told in third-person point of view, using words like *she*, *he*, and *them*. They should be unbiased and only give the facts, with no opinions or emotions of the author involved. Biographers do reveal emotions of the person being written about when the emotions can be documented. Allow students to write a rough draft in their journals, and then turn in a final draft on a separate sheet.
- **Writing an autobiography:** Then, have students return to their partners and switch handouts and timelines. Have students write paragraph-long autobiographies. Remind students that autobiographies are told from first-person point of view, using words like *I*, *me*, *we*, and *us*, and that like biographies, autobiographies only give the facts and history of a person's life with no added emotion, thoughts, or feelings unless they are documented (e.g., through letters, testimony about behaviors that others give, etc.).

10. Display students' biographies and autobiographies side-by-side around the room. Ask: *What are the main differences between an autobiography and a biography?* Give students a few minutes to examine the biographies and autobiographies of their classmates. As they look at the examples, have them complete Handout 5.2 Biography Versus Autobiography. An answer key is provided (Appendix B2).
11. Discuss how the biographies and autobiographies are alike and how they differ. Discuss the correct answers to the handout. Ask: *What are the advantages of reading a biography versus reading an autobiography? What are the advantages of reading an autobiography versus a biography?*

HANDOUT 5.1

INTERVIEW AN EXPERT

Directions: Interview a classmate. Take notes below about your classmate's answers, but do not try to write every word your classmate says. Write just enough to help you remember the responses.

1. What is your full name?
2. When were you born?
3. How old are you?
4. Tell me about your family.
5. Do you have any pets?
6. Tell me about your best friends.
7. What do you enjoy doing?

HANDOUT 5.1, CONTINUED

8. Where do you live?

9. What is your favorite memory?

10. What is your worst memory? If you aren't comfortable sharing your worst memory with me, what is a bad memory you feel comfortable sharing?

HANDOUT 5.2

BIOGRAPHY VERSUS AUTOBIOGRAPHY

Directions: For each statement below, mark whether it is a characteristic of biography, autobiography, or both.

1. Written from first-person point of view. ________
2. Written from third-person point of view. ________
3. Uses words like "me," "I," "us," and "we." ________
4. Uses words like "he," "she," "they," and "you." ________
5. The author is writing about him- or herself. ________
6. The author is writing about another real individual. ________
7. Nonfiction and informational in nature. ________
8. Presents events in chronological order. ________
9. Provides factual information about a real individual. ________
10. Highlights the most important parts of an individual's life. ________
11. Does not have bias, emotion, or opinion. ________
12. Provides an overview of an individual's history/life events. ________

LESSON

6 Introduction to Memoir

MATERIALS

- Student journals
- Three pictures (magazine shots of familiar objects, places, or people will do) from different shots or lenses (long shot, close-up, etc.)
- Video: "Jacqueline Woodson Reads from Her Memoir *Brown Girl Dreaming*" (available at https://www.youtube.com/watch?v=b5P3Y06co54)
- Handout 6.1: Formative Assessment 2
- Appendix B3: Formative Assessment 2 Answer Key

- Perspective and purpose affect how we write and how we read the work of others.
- Experience shapes identity.
- Unique points of view are shaped by unique life experiences.

OBJECTIVES

Students will:

- develop skills in looking for details that reflect moments in their lives, and
- explore and describe memoir.

- Memoir
- Memory
- Memoirist

SEQUENCE

WARM UP

1. Ask students to identify the three nonfiction genres discussed so far in the unit (biography, autobiography, and informational text). Ask students if they can identify one more genre of nonfiction. If students identified memoir on their preassessment or in previous lessons, guide them to recall this answer. Ask: *Can you think of one more form of nonfiction that is based on specific memories?*

INSTRUCTION: MEMOIR

2. Ask: *Where do we get ideas for memoirs?* Write responses on the board. Encourage students to think back to the timeline of important events in their lives as possible memoir ideas. Ask students to categorize the types of important events. Students should understand that memoirs are often written about:
   - ✓ an event/time period that was joyous or exciting,
   - ✓ an event/time period that was sad or frightening,
   - ✓ an emotionally-charged or life-altering experience,
   - ✓ an event that taught the writer a lesson or changed the writer in some way, or
   - ✓ a memory that explores a meaningful past relationship.

   Students should understand that memoirists often write about memories associated with poignant events that they can recall with clarity. Add *memory* and *memoirist* to the word wall.
3. Ask students if they think a memoir gives a full history of a person's life. (No.) Memoir is a special type of nonfiction because it is a story based on a memory that retells a real-life event or point in history. Memoir has all of the story elements of a fictional story, such as setting, characters, conflict, and plot. Tell students that, by the end of the unit, they will create a memoir that will contain the best style elements of fiction, but will still be nonfiction.
4. Read the following Tennessee Williams (1999) quote to students:

   > The scene is memory and is therefore nonrealistic. Memory takes a lot of poetic licence. It omits some details; others are exaggerated, according to the emotional value of the articles it touches, for memory is seated predominantly in the heart. (p. 3)

5. Ask students to turn to a shoulder partner and discuss their thoughts about the quote. Ask: *What can you conclude about the nature of memoirs? What can you conclude about the role of perspective in memoir? Are memoirs always accurate? Are biographies and autobiographies always accurate? Based on the quote, what reason might someone have for tweaking the truth in a work of nonfiction, in a memoir? Should an author knowingly distort the truth or insert untrue information?*
6. Engage students in a discussion about what features make a memoir different from biography. Essentially, biographies and autobiographies are documented sequences of events in a person's life, whereas a memoir is a personal reflection of a more limited time period.
7. Using the three pictures brought to class (magazine shots of familiar objects, places, or people will do), ask students how the shots are different. Introduce the terms long shot, medium shot, and close up. Tell students that they will (1) learn how to look at a memory from the perspective of a long shot, medium shot, and close up; (2) learn how to select a topic for their own memoir; (3) look at it through a specific lens; and (4) closely focus on and examine that event or memory. Guide students to seeing the camera shot as a metaphor for how they can look at their own memories. Ask for examples.

READ ALOUD

8. Show students the video of Jacqueline Woodson reading from *Brown Girl Dreaming*. Ask: *Why did the author write this story? What memory or memories does she focus on? What makes it so powerful? Have you ever had a memory that has changed over time? How did your perspective change what the memory meant to you?*

ACTIVITY: AN IMPORTANT MEMORY TO ME

9. Explain that memoirs are often very personal writing experiences because the authors often include life-changing events. Tell students: *Think about a story you remember involving a holiday, birthday, or family or school event, etc., that tells us how you feel about your experiences growing up.* Give students time to reflect for a moment.
10. Then, ask students to write a journal entry describing the event they have recalled. If there is time, students who are willing to share their entries can share with a shoulder partner.

> Remind students that memoir involves personal writing experiences. Students will be exploring past experiences, feelings, and emotions. Encourage students to be open and honest because this will help ensure that their writing is rich and compelling, but they should never feel like they need to write about topics that they feel are too personal or painful. They should also be very respectful of others' work.

PREPARATION: FORMATIVE ASSESSMENT 2

11. Administer Formative Assessment 2 (Handout 6.1). An answer key is provided (Appendix B4).

12. **Using the assessment data:** Determine whether there is any content you have taught so far that you need to review or reinforce. For example, you might find a group of students having trouble differentiating between different genres or distinguishing characteristics of memoir. Plan to provide a mini-lesson at a convenient time to ensure these students understand the concepts before going forward.

HANDOUT 6.1

FORMATIVE ASSESSMENT 2

Directions: Answer the following questions about biography and memoir.

1. What is nonfiction?

2. What is a memoir?

3. What is a biography?

4. Identify these following as being B (biography) or (M) memoir.
   a. ________ I took a deep breath, clenched my teeth, and jumped off the dock. The water hit me like a thousand tiny needles, chilling me to the bone.
   b. ________ Ben was born in 1990. He lived with his parents and two sisters. Ben loved to play soccer and watch movies. He wanted to be an astronaut when he grew up.
   c. ________ Margaret lived on Cherry Hill Road. She loved to read and studied hard. She knew hard work would bring her closer to her goal of being a doctor. In 2015, she was accepted into medical school. Her dream was coming true.
   d. ________ "Ouch!" I yelled, and I slapped my arm hard. I heard the angry buzzing as the yellow jacket flew away. My arm began to throb as a rosy pink color spread where I had been stung.

HANDOUT 6.1, CONTINUED

5. How are memoirs and biographies different from informational text?

6. Explain the difference between an autobiography and a biography.

LESSON 7 Focusing on a Memory, Event, or Relationship

MATERIALS

- ✓ Teacher's copy of a selected work by Cynthia Rylant (e.g. "My Grandmother's Hair," *The Relatives Came, When I Was Young in the Mountains,* etc.)
- ✓ Teacher's copy of "My Approach" by Marion Roach Smith (available at http://marionroach.com/writing-help/approach)
- ✓ Butcher paper (one large piece per student)
- ✓ Appendix B4: Focus on the Rubric, Part 1

- Perspective and purpose affect how we write and how we read the work of others.
- We understand ourselves better when we work to make sense of our own experiences and the experiences of others.

OBJECTIVES

Students will:

- ✓ analyze memoirs for elements of story, and
- ✓ write about a meaningful memory, event (time period), or relationship.

- Figurative language
- Metaphor
- Simile

SEQUENCE

READ ALOUD

1. Invite students to find a comfortable place for listening. Ask students to reflect on the focus of a memoir. When a photographer takes snapshots, they look into the camera and focus on just the person, place, or thing they are taking a picture of; everything else is less important. Memoirists do the same: They sharpen the focus of their story by exploring just one event (or time period), memory, or relationship.
2. Read aloud a selected text by Cynthia Rylant. Her work is particularly exemplary in its use of figurative language, which makes her stories compelling. Ask: *What is the term we use to describe how authors compare two different objects or ideas?* (Metaphors and similes.) Ask students to identify any figurative language in the selected text. For example, in "My Grandmother's Hair," the author uses a simile to compare her grandmother's hair to her writing ability. Add *figurative language* and *simile* to the word wall.

- **Focus on the rubric:** Display the first part of the Memoir Anthology Rubric (Appendix B5: Focus on the Rubric, Part 1).
- As a class, decide how one of Cynthia Rylant's texts fits into this rubric. Ask: *Does the story focus on one meaningful memory, event (time period), or relationship? Is the memoirist's connection to that memory or relationship reinforced throughout the whole story? Does the memoirist discuss why that relationship or memory was so important to her?*
- Ask students to hold up their fingers to show the points they would give the story if using this rubric. If there is disagreement among students, engage them in a discussion about why they gave a particular rating to see if the class can come to consensus.

ACTIVITY: BODYSTORMING

3. Introduce "My Approach" by Marion Roach Smith. Read aloud her "The Memoir Manifesto."
4. Remind students: *Where do we get ideas for memoirs?* Encourage students to think back to the timelines they created as possible memoir ideas to identify 2–3 ideas they might write about in a memoir.
5. Distribute butcher paper. Ask students to think about a part of their body that represents something important, valued, or unique about them (i.e., if a student plays basketball, a hand is important for dribbling; if a student dances, feet are important for movement; if a student enjoys singing, a mouth/throat/face is important for producing sound, etc.).

6. Ask: *What is a part of your body that is important to whom you are as an individual? Be creative!* Have students trace a silhouette of that body part on their butcher paper. Emphasize that there are no right or wrong answers, but they should provide a good reason for their selections.
7. Ask: *What does your silhouette say about you? What does this body part represent?* Have students to do a "brain dump." Encourage students to take their pencil, and, inside the silhouette, start writing about the body part they selected. Tell students this is where, as a memoirist, they will begin closely examining one important aspect of their life in greater depth.

During the brain dump, emphasize that students do not need to think logically or in sequence: Students are not required to write in complete sentences, but can write words, phrases, dialogue, bullet points, or even draw pictures that they associate with the silhouette.

Students should include information about why they selected that particular body part, how it is used, any past stories that are associated with it, any emotions associated with it, and why it has such value. Tell students to allow their minds to roam freely from memory to memory, and to not lift their pencil from the paper, but to write continuously until they are told to stop.

8. After about 5 minutes, ask students to stop writing and look at their silhouette. Give students a few minutes to examine and reflect on the words and phrases that they wrote. Remind students that often times, memoirs grow from a specific event, memory, or center around one important thing. Ask: *Is there a story here? Does the actual part of your body serve as a metaphor or simile for something else, something deeper? What is it?*

Remind students that their memoir idea may change over the next few lessons. If students struggle with this activity, or if you feel it may be useful, consider repeating this activity in later lessons.

CLOSE

9. In their journals, have students draw a line down the center of the page. Using the information that they wrote in their silhouettes, encourage students to write down a possible story idea for their memoir. On the left, they should write a bulleted summary of the events that surround that memory in chronological order. On the right, they should write the emotions and thoughts associated with each event.

LESSON 8 Examining an Event

MATERIALS

- ✓ Teacher's copy of the first 12 paragraphs of *A Girl From Yamhill* by Beverly Cleary (also available at http://www.barnesandnoble.com/w/girl-from-yamhill-beverly-cleary/1102960752)
- ✓ Large white paper (one per student)
- ✓ White paper (two per student)
- ✓ Rubber band
- ✓ Sticky notes
- ✓ Appendix B5: Focus on the Rubric, Part 2

Perspective and purpose affect how we write and how we read other's work.

OBJECTIVES

Students will:

- ✓ use memoirs to closely examine the details of an event or time period in one's life; and
- ✓ identify the emotional journey presented in a memoir.

- Main idea
- Supporting details
- Emotional journey

SEQUENCE

READ ALOUD

1. Read aloud the excerpt from *A Girl From Yamhill.* Ask: *What events did this story examine? If you were (someone else) in this story, and you were to tell this story, how would it be different? If the author were to look back on this event, do you think the memory would evoke as much emotion as he or she was feeling at that moment in the story?*

ACTIVITY: EXPANDING AN EVENT

2. Explain that sometimes memoirists take a single event and elaborate or expand upon it (stretch a rubber band for a visual). Explain that in order to elaborate or expand on a story, students need to ask themselves: *What details would give the reader insight into the kind of person you were prior to the event? What beliefs or knowledge did you have?* (Stretch the rubber band again.) *What happened after the event, once you were able to reflect back on it? Did you change as a person or learn a lesson? Did you acquire new knowledge or beliefs as a result of the event?* (Have the rubber band go back to its normal size.) The various emotions evoked in a character as a result of a memorable event are known as an emotional journey. Add this word to the word wall.
3. Distribute a large piece of white paper to each student. Ask students to think about a time when they had a strong emotional response to something in their life—happy, frustrated, excited, sad, etc. Ask students to think of a time when a character they read about in a book had such an event occur (one that evoked a strong emotion). Write these examples on the board. Encourage students to think of an emotional experience they have not yet described in this unit.

Allow students a few minutes to work on one of the following tasks:

- **Option A:** Students should divide the paper into three columns. In the center, they should describe their personal experience and draw an illustration depicting that event. Then, they should create a comic strip of the events that occurred. For each panel, they should expand upon the details of it and record these supporting details in their journal.
- **Option B:** Students should assume the role of their favorite book character and choose one event or memory they believe was an emotional moment for the character. They should write a description of the event and a description of why it was important to the character. Then, they should write a description of what happened before and after the event to make it memorable.

ACTIVITY: ADDING SUPPORTING DETAILS

4. Ask students to think about the event they picked and all of the details—both physical descriptions and emotional responses—that help make that memory stand out to them. To continue examining an event, students must think about all of the little details. Just like zooming in with a camera can help a photographer see the little details in a picture, focusing on a single event can help a writer see the tiny and vivid details that help make up that memory. These details are called *supporting details.* They help support the story and make it stronger by adding more information, description, and background. Add *supporting details* to the word wall.
5. Distribute sticky notes to each student. Ask students to write one detail per sticky note, sticking the notes to each section of their comics or written descriptions. Tell students to include details that give sensory information and to add as many supporting details as possible.
6. Have students read through their sticky notes and think about how their feelings or the feelings of the character they chose changed during the event: *What emotional journey did they have?*
7. Using the sticky notes, ask students to identify their (or the character's) emotional journey as it relates to the event (e.g., *I was fearful and nervous about performing in front of an audience. I bravely walked out onto the stage. After performing, I was elated and proud of myself!*). *What did they (or their character) learn about themselves after the event? How did they grow as an individual?* Remind students that they can feel many emotions throughout the unfolding of the event.

ACTIVITY: EXAMINING AN OBJECT

8. Reiterate that a photographer's job is to capture and record a important event or big story. For example, a photographer may take a picture of a tree, but may then want to take a closer look at the branches or leaves, or where a squirrel is hiding. Depending on the photographer's perspective, the story may be different.
9. Distribute a sheet of paper to each student. Ask students to roll their paper like a telescope. Model for students how a photographer would take a lens and zoom in for a long shot, mid-shot, and close-up shot by twisting the paper to elongate the paper telescope as needed. Inform students that they may need to move closer to the object as they examine it.
10. Distribute another sheet of paper to each student. Ask them to fold the paper in half horizontally, and then to fold it again into thirds, so that when the paper is unfolded, there are six equal folds (three on top, three on bottom). Ask students to label the top three and bottom three boxes

long shot, mid-shot, and close-up. Then, have students fold the paper in half again along the crease so that just the top three boxes are visible for now.

11. Have the class roam outside, in the hallway, or throughout the classroom with their telescopes. Ask students to observe the concrete objects and people around them, and find one object to focus on. Ask: *What is happening? What can you physically see? How does that object change as you move from a long shot to a close-up shot? What can you observe about this object using your five senses?* Students should also describe the object during each stage using the five senses and including as much sensory detail as possible.
12. Return to the classroom and allow students to share their findings. Guide students to the understanding that different viewpoints and perspectives can completely change the way something looks and how others perceive it. In the same way, a single event can have different stories based on who is telling the story: An outside character often has a long shot picture of the event, looking from the outside in, whereas an inside character is often able to more closely examine the event and experience things on a much deeper level.

ACTIVITY: EXAMINING AN EXPERIENCE

13. Ask students to unfold their paper so that the bottom three boxes are visible. Have them close their eyes and think about the event that they wrote about earlier in the lesson. Ask: *How might that event look to an outsider who only has a long-shot view? How might it look to people who are involved, but only have a mid-shot view? Finally, how might that event look to you now that you have considered the close-up shot? What emotions and thoughts are felt that others without the close perspective do not have? What is the story within the story?*
14. Then, encourage students to draw the three different lenses on their paper, and to write a brief explanation of each perspective in each box, listing the names of the people who would have those views in the event they selected to write about.

> This exercise may seem very abstract and difficult to some students. You may need to give an example of their classroom and ask how a person walking by the door might describe students working on a lesson in the classroom, how the teacher might describe students working on a lesson in the classroom, and how a student might describe their own experiences working on the lesson.

CLOSE

- **Focus on the rubric:** Display the second part of the Memoir Anthology Rubric (Appendix B5: Focus on the Rubric, Part 2).
- As a class, decide how the Cleary excerpt fits into this rubric: What single event or memory did the author examine? Does the story have enough detail to give the reader a full idea of what happened and how the author responded?
- Ask students to hold up their fingers to show the points they would give (the story) if using this rubric. If there is disagreement among students, engage them in a discussion about why they gave a particular rating to see if the class can come to consensus.

LESSON

9 Showing, Not Telling

MATERIALS

- ✓ Teacher's copy of "Writing Guide: Descriptive & Sensory Detail" (available at http://www.wright.edu/~david.wilson/eng1100/sensorydetails.pdf)
- ✓ Teacher's copy of "Where I'm From" by George Ella Lyon (available at http://www.georgeellalyon.com/where.html)
- ✓ Student computer and Internet access to "One Step at a Time" by Anant Vinjamoori (available at http://teacher.scholastic.com/writeit/criticspicks/memoir/AnantV-OneStep.htm)
- ✓ Handout 9.1: Sensory Details
- ✓ Handout 9.2: Formative Assessment 3
- ✓ Appendix B6: Focus on the Rubric, Part 3

- Perspective and purpose affect how we write and how we read the work of others.
- Experience shapes identity.
- We understand ourselves better when we work to make sense of our own experiences and the experiences of others.

OBJECTIVES

Students will:

- ✓ use compelling language when writing a memoir,
- ✓ analyze memoirs for evidence or clues as to the author's character and purpose for writing, and
- ✓ understand the concept of using sensory language to create powerful writing.

- Sensory details
- Adjectives
- Images
- Reflect

SEQUENCE

WARM UP

1. Display and read aloud the following quote by E. L. Doctorow: "Good writing is supposed to evoke sensation in the reader. Not the fact that it is raining, but the feeling of being rained upon."
2. Ask: *What do you think this quote means?* Have students write a paragraph-long journal entry analyzing the quote. Then, allow volunteers to share what they have written and discuss as a class.
3. Ask: *What are our five senses?* Tell students to keep them in mind as you read a passage aloud.
4. Read aloud "Example Text: Paragraph Without Sensory Detail" (Passage A) from "Writing Guide: Descriptive & Sensory Detail." Ask students to think about which senses were described as you read the passage. Tell them to hold on to their thoughts or jot them down to share with the class after you've read another passage.
5. Read aloud "Example Text: Add Sight" (Passage B). Be sure to read Passage B in the same tone as Passage A so students focus only on the writing, not the intonation.
6. Ask students to think about which senses were invoked as you read Passage B and discuss with a partner how each passage made them feel. If they felt differently after Passage B, what characteristics of the writing do they believe contributed to that? What were the similarities and differences between the two passages? Do they believe one passage was written more skillfully than the other? Come together as a whole class and have students discuss their thoughts.
7. Guide students to the conclusion that good writing is supposed to make readers feel emotion or describe things in such a way that readers actually feel like they are a part of the story. Because the author cannot physically make readers feel things, like being rained on, the author has to describe what the rain feels like, how it smells, where the rain is falling, etc. These details are called *sensory details* because they appeal to readers' senses. Add this phrase to the word wall.

ACTIVITY: USING SENSORY DETAILS

8. Divide students into two groups based on Formative Assessment 2.

- **Group A:** Students should have a strong understanding of characteristics of memoir, such as emphasis on emotion. In groups of 2–3, students should write a page-long description of a rainstorm, hike in the woods, swim in the ocean, or other sensory experience. Ask students to add as many examples of sensory details, adjectives, and figurative language as possible, painting a picture in readers' minds. Ask: *How did the rain feel? How did it taste? What did it sound like?* Add *adjective* to the word wall.
- **Group B:** Students might still be struggling to distinguish between memoir and autobiography. Distribute Handout 9.1: Sensory Details to groups of 2–3. In the left column, groups should list the five senses. Ask students to think about the last time they were in a rainstorm, or on a hike in the woods, or swimming at the ocean, etc. Beside each of the five senses, ask students to use adjectives and sensory details to describe the rain (or ocean, woods, etc.) for each of the senses. Finally, they should write a paragraph-long description using the adjectives and sensory details they wrote down.

9. Afterward, allow groups to share their writing. Create a master list of especially poignant adjectives and descriptions.
10. Ask: *Why do we have so many different descriptions of similar things?* Students should understand that sensory events can be described very differently based on a person's experiences and point of view. Some students may be describing a light rain or a drizzle, while others may be remembering a thunderstorm. Ask: *If I were to ask each of you to give one sensory word to describe how you feel about Halloween, do you think you would all have the same word? What do you think would happen (many very different responses)? Why? Let's try.*
11. Tell students that these sensory details are particularly powerful because they help "show," not "tell," the story. Readers are able to create a mental image, or smell or sense of touch, as they read. Add *image* to the word wall.
12. Ask students to close their eyes and try to form an image in their mind based on two short descriptions. Say: *It was raining and I was sad because I wanted to go outside and play.* Then, pause and say: *I heaved a huge sigh and looked out the window gloomily. The rain was hurling itself at the window and pooling in the street. I could not go outside to play.* Ask: *Which sensory details helped you form the most powerful image in your mind? Which sentences simply told what happened? Which sentence showed what happened? What words in particular helped you form a powerful image in your mind?*

As students write, encourage them to use their bodies as a "reference point," as Artis Henderson said,

> to recreate what was happening inside [their] own frame during the moment [they are] describing. Were my shoulders tense? Did my fingertips smell like oranges? Was my breathing jagged? These personal sensory details are the key to delivering the most powerful, immediate experience to the reader—and isn't that why we're here? (as cited in Roach Smith, 2014)

Ask students what is meant when we say a piece of writing is "powerful."

READ ALOUD

13. Read aloud "Where I'm From" by George Ella Lyon.
14. Ask: *How did the author use sensory details to describe what she came from? How is the phrase "I am from clothespins, from Clorox and carbon-*

tetrachloride" more compelling than simply saying, "I remember doing the laundry"? What does it mean to say "I am from . . ."? What images and sensory details were particularly poignant for you?

15. Reiterate that memoirists must critically reflect on their experiences and who they are. Ask: *What do you think it means to reflect?* When they reflect on themselves, students should understand that means taking a closer look at themselves.
16. Say: *When you look at your reflection in the mirror, you can see the little nuances, or things that make your face what it is—the size of your nose, the color of your eyes, your skin type, freckles, moles—things you wouldn't see immediately if you weren't looking closely. The same is true for reflecting on yourself: When you critically examine your life, you can more easily see what makes you who you are as a person, and can identify the little nuances, memories, events, people, and relationships that make you who you are.*
17. Add *reflect* to the word wall.
18. Have students refer back to their timeline sentence strips and select one of their events. Ask them to think about what they saw, smelled, felt, tasted, or heard at the time of the event. Give students 5–10 minutes to write in their journals with as many sensory details as possible. Students should also try to describe the emotions they experienced. If they choose an event they have written about before, be sure they are adding greater detail.
19. Afterward, students who are willing should read aloud their writings to the class. They should give their classmates the opportunity to interview them, asking them why they picked certain sensory details and what significance they have for the writer. Ask if the story might have been remembered differently if another person had told it. Prompt students to also consider: *Are there any particularly powerful images that the student created? What sensory details really stand out? What effect did those images have on you as he or she read them aloud? Why do you think he or she chose these particular sensory details and emotions to describe?*

CLOSE

- **Focus on the rubric:** Display the third part of the Memoir Anthology Rubric (Appendix B5: Focus on the Rubric, Part 3).
- As a class, decide how "Where I'm From" fits into this rubric: Does the poem include sensory details, images, and descriptions?
- Ask students to hold up their fingers to show the points they would give (the poem) if using this rubric. If there is disagreement among students, engage them in a discussion about why they gave a particular rating to see if the class can come to consensus.

PREPARATION: FORMATIVE ASSESSMENT 3

20. Administer Formative Assessment 3 (Handout 9.2). Students will need computer access to read "One Step at a Time" by Anant Vinjamoori.
21. **Using the assessment data:** Determine whether there is any content that you need to review or reinforce. For example, you might find a group of students still struggling with what a memoir is and how to write one. Provide a mini-lesson at a convenient time to ensure these students understand the concepts before going forward.

Emphasize to students that the picture or story must illustrate a meaningful event that they experienced *personally*. A picture of someone else or an event that the student did not experience will not produce a strong memory, and will not be useful for the upcoming activity.

HOMEWORK

22. Ask students to bring in a photograph of themselves that shows an important event or represents a special and meaningful memory. Alternatively, students can draw a picture of themselves.

HANDOUT 9.1

SENSORY DETAILS

Directions: Think about the last time you were at the beach, hiking, or caught in the rain, etc. In the left column, list the five senses. In the right column, use adjectives and sensory details to describe your experience.

Senses	Adjectives and Sensory Details

HANDOUT 9.2

FORMATIVE ASSESSMENT 3

Directions: Answer the following questions about memoir. Use a separate sheet of paper if necessary.

1. What makes a memoir different from other types of nonfiction?

2. Explain the difference between sequencing and examining a single event.

3. Explain the techniques writers use to examine, elaborate, and expand on the details of a single event.

4. What are memoirs usually about?

HANDOUT 9.2, CONTINUED

5. Read "One Step at a Time" by Anant Vinjamoori (available at http://teacher.scholastic.com/writeit/criticspicks/memoir/AnantV-OneStep.htm). Then, answer the following questions.
   a. What is the primary external event in this memoir?
   b. Summarize the internal events in the memoir in your own words.
   c. Use the following section of the Memoir Anthology Rubric to grade the memoir you just read. What number would you assign it? Justify your response.

Memoir Anthology Rubric	**1 Memoirist Needing Retraining**	**2 Memoirist in Training**	**3 Amateur Memoirist**	**4 Professional Memoirist**
Closely examines a period of time or single event, and supports the main event with details.	Story is not about a focused time or event, but many larger, unrelated stories or sequences of events.	Story examines a period of time or a single event, but does not include detail that gives any meaning and understanding of the event and the author's response.	Story examines a period of time or a single event, but lacks sufficient detail to give more than bare bones meaning and understanding of the event and the author's response.	Story examines a period of time or a single event, adding ample detail to give full meaning and understanding of the event and the author's response.

LESSON

10 Framing Your Topic

MATERIALS

- Student journals
- White paper (one per student)
- Colored pens or markers

- Perspective and purpose affect how we write and how we read the work of others.
- Experience shapes identity.
- We understand ourselves better when we work to make sense of our own experiences and the experiences of others.

OBJECTIVES

Students will:

- distinguish between the different nonfiction genres—biography, autobiography, memoir, and informational text; and
- identify the importance of framing a story.

- Frame
- External events
- Internal events

SEQUENCE

WARM UP

1. Ask students to identify the four types of nonfiction that have been discussed in class (i.e., biography, autobiography, memoir, and informational text). Ask students to pick which kind of nonfiction they

would like to write and place them in four groups according to their preferences.

2. Distribute an index card to each group. On the front of each card, students should work together to write the name of the genre and a bulleted list of the characteristics of that genre. Each group should work together to form one list per group. Then, each student should write a short paragraph in that genre about the first day of school.
3. Afterward, have students read their group's short writings aloud. Students should evaluate the degree to which each of the criteria of the genre has been included in the shared piece. Ask: *Which of the characteristics of a (memoir, biography, or informational piece) have the authors included in this piece? What is missing?*

ACTIVITY: PHOTOGRAPH

4. Distribute paper. Have students to place their photos/drawings in the center. The white space around the photo will serve as a frame. Explain to students that one powerful thing about memoirs is that they often tell a story within a story. Using a colored pencil or marker, ask students to write down all of the external events that they can physically *see* happening in their picture (e.g., blowing out candles on a birthday cake, people clapping) and then describe them using sensory details in a different colored pencil or marker (e.g., the roar of the crowd, the sweet taste of the cake). Students should write around the photo, filling the frame. Encourage students to use sensory details and colorful adjectives and to fill up as much of the blank space as possible. Then, have students remove their pictures to reveal the white space in the center of the frame. Ask them to think about what may be happening in the picture that is unseen (e.g., how they felt before or after blowing out the candles). They should write these internal events (thoughts and emotions) inside the frame and then replace the picture, illustrating internal and external events.
5. Afterward, explain that narratives can contain *external events, internal events,* or both. Point out that external events include events, problems, and solutions, whereas internal events include feelings and experiences. Ask: *Based on the memoirs we've read so far, which type of event do you think is emphasized in a memoir?*
6. Tell students that even though memoirs emphasize internal events, they are typically started by an external event. What makes memoirs unique is that they look beyond the events that are physically happening and can be seen, and focus on what is emotionally happening to the author during that moment, or the unseen—the experiences, feelings, and emotions that occur in that one moment. These events will become

powerful if they are described using sensory details that appeal to readers' senses and draw them into the story.

7. Add *external events* and *internal events* to the word wall.
8. In the same way, how a writer frames a story can create a desired response from readers. Ask: *Imagine you want to ask your parents if you can go outside to play. How you frame that question, and the information you use to support your question plays a large role in how they will respond. For example, how would your parents respond to "Can I go outside even though I have a big test tomorrow?" versus "I have cleaned my room and done all my homework, so can I go outside?"* Point out that both questions are asking the same thing, but the information that was used to frame the question caused a specific response.
9. Display a photo of the ocean. Placing that photograph in a beautiful, complementary frame and hanging it on the wall would make it even more appealing, whereas an ugly, clashing frame can lessen the appeal of the picture, making it seem less desirable. Consult a museum's website (complete a virtual tour of the National Gallery of Art at http://www.nga.gov/exhibitions/webtours.shtm) to show how frames are used to complement the artist's work. It is still the same picture in both cases, but how it is presented can affect how the viewer responds to it.
10. Memoirists think about what they want the reader to learn or take away from the story, and then frame the memoir using internal and external events. Ask: *What do you want your reader to learn from the memoir you will write? How will you plan to use sensory detail to support your readers in understanding your theme and purpose?* Encourage students to jot down some ideas in their journals.

PREPARATION: FOR NEXT LESSON

11. At this point in the unit, it is important that students are developing a strong understanding of the elements and characteristics of memoir. As students are writing in their journals, review journal entries. Also, let students know that if they have any concerns or confusion about unit vocabulary or concepts, that you are available to discuss and clarify any concerns. Remind students that as you get closer to writing memoirs, you want to be sure students feel confident about their own learning and ability to write a powerful memoir.

LESSON 11 What's the Point?

MATERIALS

- ✓ Teacher's copy of "Fish Cheeks" by Amy Tan (available at https://www.commonlit.org/texts/fish-cheeks)
- ✓ Student computer and Internet access to "Fish Cheeks" by Amy Tan (available at https://www.commonlit.org/texts/fish-cheeks)
- ✓ Student journals
- ✓ Highlighters
- ✓ Handout 11.1 Finding Textual Evidence and Making Inferences
- ✓ Appendix B7: Focus on the Rubric, Part 4

- Perspective and purpose affect how we write and how we read the work of others.
- Experience shapes identity.
- We understand ourselves better when we work to make sense of our own experiences and the experiences of others.

OBJECTIVES

Students will:

- ✓ analyze memoirs for evidence or clues as to the author's character and purpose for writing; and
- ✓ identify the emotional journey presented in a memoir.

- Textual evidence
- Inference
- Character traits
- Author's purpose
- Theme

SEQUENCE

READ ALOUD

1. Read aloud "Fish Cheeks" by Amy Tan. Ask students: *Have you ever had a similar experience to Amy's? Have you ever been embarrassed by a family tradition? Have you ever been embarrassed by an event in your past?*
2. Tell students that sometimes, the best memoirs come from difficult or painful memories. Remind them that when they are in the moment, sometimes a particular event can seem incredibly big, life changing, and horrible. Ask students to identify the event in "Fish Cheeks" that was especially life changing or horrible.
3. Ask: *What often happens to the way you feel about past horrible or painful events after time has passed and you have stepped out of that particular moment? How did Amy feel about this event after time passed? What did Amy say?* (She was able to "appreciate her lesson and the true purpose behind our particular menu.") *Can what seems like a horrible event at one time later be viewed as an overall worthwhile experience*? Ask students to share similar experiences where the passage of time has changed their perceptions.

ACTIVITY: AN EMBARRASSING EVENT

4. In their journals, have students write about a time they were embarrassed. Encourage students to think of a more recent embarrassing memory, because the closer the memoirist is to the experience, the larger and more vivid the details and emotions are in their mind. Or, ask students to close their eyes and try to relive a particular past embarrassing memory, thinking about how they felt, and the sensory images and details that were present during that time. Ask students to put themselves back into that particular moment and expand it again.
5. If time permits, allow students to share with a shoulder partner, but emphasize that students do not have to share if the memory is too embarrassing or personal.

ACTIVITY: ANALYZING A MEMOIRIST

6. Revisit "Fish Cheeks." Remind students that memoirs are stories that closely examine a single event or memory. Ask: *What memory did this story examine?* Point out that this author took something as simple as a dinner, and transformed it into an emotional story. A good memoirist will not simply tell the reader about himself or herself, but will weave

details into the story that show or give the reader hints as to what the character is like.

7. This information is called textual evidence. When a writer does not directly say something but implies it, the reader must make an *inference*, or use what the reader already knows about something plus *textual evidence* to prove something. Ask: *For example, when the story says "Robert grimaced," what can the reader infer?* (Robert was feeling upset or uncomfortable.) *Did the author explicitly say this?* (No.) *Then why do we believe Robert was upset?* (Even though the author never explicitly revealed Robert's emotions, we can take what we know about grimacing and infer that it is the outward display of discomfort or distress.) Add *inference* and *textual evidence* to the word wall.
8. Divide the class into groups of 2–3 based on Formative Assessment 3.

> The first two paragraphs of "Fish Cheeks" contain the most concrete and specific character traits and details, the middle section requires more inference and abstract thought, and the final three paragraphs require the deepest analysis.

- **Group A:** Students demonstrated strong skills in their memoir analysis on the assessment. They will work with the last three paragraphs of "Fish Cheeks."
- **Group B:** Students demonstrated moderate skills in heir memoir analysis. They will work with the middle three paragraphs of the story.
- **Group C:** Students demonstrated limited or developing skills in their memoir analysis. They will work with the first two paragraphs of the story.

9. Have groups read their assigned passages together, thinking about what the story tells the reader about memoirist Amy Tan: *Through what lens is this story being told? Ask students to highlight information in their passages that either gives textual evidence or inferential evidence as to her character.*
10. Distribute Handout 11.1: Finding Textual Evidence and Making Inferences. Students should record textual evidence on the left and make interpretations on the right.

INSTRUCTION: CHARACTER WEB

11. Create a character web on the board, writing the name "Amy" in the center and circling it. Ask each group to share what they learned about Amy in their analysis sections. If another student disagrees with the analysis, ask the group to prove its claim using the textual evidence from its first column. While students are sharing, draw lines from Amy's name and write the information about her onto the character web.
12. Tell students they are going to dig deeper into Amy's character to find some words to describe her personality, or character traits (e.g., jealous, kind, impatient, etc.). Ask: *Are character traits external or internal?*

Students should understand that character traits can tell what the character is like on the inside, including how the character thinks, acts, and feels. Add *character traits* to the word wall.

13. Have students list Amy's character traits. Add them to the character web using a different colored marker.

ACTIVITY: THEMES AND LESSONS LEARNED

14. Say: *Now that we know more about Amy's character, think about her reason for writing this memoir.* Remind students that authors always have a reason or purpose for writing. This is known as the author's purpose. Ask: *What is the purpose of a memoir?* (To entertain, to teach a lesson, to share experiences, to inform, etc.) *What can we learn from a memoir?* (The story usually centers on a theme, or message, with the author sharing a lesson that he or she learned.) Add *author's purpose* and *theme* to the word wall.
15. Reread the ending of "Fish Cheeks," beginning with "After everyone had gone . . ." Ask: *What was Amy's purpose in writing this memoir? What was the theme? What lesson did Amy learn that she is trying to share with us?* Have students share their responses in their journals.

CLOSE

- **Focus on the rubric:** Display the first part of the Memoir Anthology Rubric (Appendix B7: Focus on the Rubric, Part 4).
- As a class, decide how "Fish Cheeks" fits into this rubric. Ask: *Is the theme or lesson clear? Is it reinforced through the story? Does the story match the lesson that was learned?*
- Ask students to hold up their fingers to show the points they would give the story if using this rubric. If there is disagreement among students, engage them in a discussion about why they gave a particular rating to see if the class can come to consensus.

HOMEWORK

16. Ask students to bring in an object that that they value or an object that they do not like but have to have. They should be willing to share the object with the class.

HANDOUT 11.1

FINDING TEXTUAL EVIDENCE AND MAKING INFERENCES

Directions: Write the exact words or evidence from the story in the "Text Evidence" box. In the "Analysis" box, interpret what you think that evidence is saying.

Textual Evidence	Analysis

LESSON

12 Author's Craft

MATERIALS

- Teacher's copy of "The Jacket" in *The Effects of Knut Hamsun on a Fresno Boy: Recollections and Essays* by Gary Soto (and also widely published in other texts and collections)
- Student computer access to memoirs (available at http://teacher.scholastic.com/writeit/readwork.asp?Genre=Memoir)
- Handout 12.1: Critiquing Memoirs
- Handout 12.2: Formative Assessment 4
- Appendix B8: Focus on the Rubric, Part 5

- We understand ourselves better when we work to make sense of our own experiences and the experiences of others.

OBJECTIVES

Students will:

- write about a meaningful memory, event (time period), or relationship;
- use dialogue to enhance writing; and
- evaluate the quality of a memoir using specific characteristics of that genre.

- Connections
- Text-to-self connection
- Dialogue
- Internal dialogue
- External dialogue

SEQUENCE

READ ALOUD

1. Read aloud "The Jacket" by Gary Soto. Ask: *Do you have a connection with Gary?* Remind students that a connection is when the reader shares an experience with the character. This is also called a *text-to-self connection*. Add this phrase to the word wall.
2. Ask students: *Have you ever been given something that you really didn't like? What was it?* Have students take out the object they were asked to bring from home. Remind students that they were able to select an object that they value or cherish, or one that, like Gary, they do not like. Divide students into groups of 3–4 based on whether they brought an object they liked or if they brought one they disliked. In their groups, encourage students to take turns explaining why they value or dislike their object. They should include the following information:
   - ✓ What object did you bring?
   - ✓ Where did you get it?
   - ✓ What is your relationship to the object (i.e., do you like/dislike it)?
   - ✓ Why did you select this object?

3. Have students write in their journals about their object and their memories associated with it. Ask: *Does this object have a story? Tell the object's story with as much detail as you can.*

ACTIVITY: READING MEMOIRS

4. Distribute Handout 12.1: Critiquing Memoirs. Have students read at least two memoirs (see Materials list) that interest them and complete the handout. (*Note.* Students have already read "One Step at a Time" by Anant Vinjamoori. They will read "Coughing and Strawberry Jam" by Milena A. in Lesson 16.) Encourage students to look for commonalities and differences between the memoirs. Students should also take note of ways that the writers craft their writing to engage the reader and ways the writers could improve.

INSTRUCTION: EXTERNAL VERSUS INTERNAL DIALOGUE

5. Explain that a memoirist can craft a story so that it seems like a conversation with the reader. One way an author can draw a reader in is by including *dialogue*. Ask: *Is dialogue internal or external in a memoir?* Add *external dialogue* and *internal dialogue* to the word wall. Guide

students to the understanding that memoirists use dialogue to show both the character's external and internal dialogue.

6. Draw an outline of a person on the board. Ask: *What would external dialogue look like?* (Speech, like talking, yelling, or whispering, that is oral or spoken aloud.) Write student responses on the outside of the person outline. Ask: *What would internal dialogue look like?* (Talking that is done inside someone's mind, like a character's thoughts, arguing with yourself, talking yourself through things, etc.) Write student responses on the inside of the person outline.

ACTIVITY: PRACTICE WITH DIALOGUE

7. Explain that there are a few rules for how to use dialogue. Ask students if they know some of the rules:
   - ✓ Writers use quotation marks to show where dialogue begins and ends.
   - ✓ Punctuation stays inside the quotation marks.
   - ✓ When using dialogue, the writer can choose to clarify who is speaking by adding a dialogue tag.
   - ✓ The first word in a quotation is always capitalized.

8. Share three examples of dialogue, one with dialogue in the beginning of the sentence, one with dialogue in the middle of the sentence, and one with dialogue at the end of a sentence. Ask students to differentiate between these examples. Dialogue tags can be added to the beginning, middle, or end of a sentence to tell the reader who is speaking. Ask students to articulate how the commas are used. (They can be used to introduce a quote or end a quote, such as in the first and second examples below, respectively.)
   - ✓ Mom said, "Come here."
   - ✓ "I don't like that," said Gary.
   - ✓ "Gross!" Gary yelled. "I hate that jacket!"

9. Divide the class into groups of 3-4 students based on the results of Formative Assessment 3.

- **Group A:** Students demonstrated high-quality writing with few or no mistakes on the paragraph-long memoir they wrote. Ask students to form a circle with the journal entry they did earlier about their object. They will pass their writing to the person on their left, who will add one sentence of dialogue to the story, taking care to revise the sentences with appropriate quotations and punctuation. When they are done, students will pass the paper again, and continue the process until every student in the group has a chance to add dialogue to their classmates' stories. When the story returns to the original author, he or she should check the suggested revisions to see if they are (a) mechanically sound (i.e., contain correct dialogue tags and punctuation) and (b) make the story more compelling.
- **Group B:** Students demonstrated moderate writing skills on the memoir they wrote. As you read "The Jacket" aloud again, ask students to identify and write sentences in which there are instances of either internal or external dialogue. Ensure that student examples use correct mechanics (i.e., correct dialogue tags and punctuation). After students have identified 10 instances of dialogue, ask students to identify ways to make the dialogue tags more compelling (i.e., instead of using the word "said," students may revise the sentences using more colorful adjectives like "barked" or "hissed").

10. Afterward, write three unpunctuated sentences with dialogue on the board. Ask for volunteers to come to the board and punctuate the sentences appropriately and correct any capitalization. Ask students to think aloud as they work, saying the reason for each form of punctuation they use and capitalization they apply.
11. Have students select one of their earlier memoir writings/drafts and add at least five sentences of dialogue.

CLOSE

- **Focus on the rubric:** Display the first part of the Memoir Anthology Rubric (Appendix B8: Focus on the Rubric, Part 5).
- As a class, decide how "The Jacket" fits into this rubric. Ask: *Does the author use ample dialogue to illustrate Gary's thoughts and emotions? Could the author provide more dialogue to further illustrate Gary's internal and external emotions?*
- Ask students to hold up their fingers to show the points they would give the story if using this rubric. If there is disagreement among students, engage them in a discussion about why they gave a particular rating to see if the class can come to consensus.

PREPARATION: FORMATIVE ASSESSMENT 4

12. Administer Formative Assessment 4 (Handout 12.2).

HANDOUT 12.1

CRITIQUING MEMOIRS

Directions: Read at least two memoirs and complete the chart for each.

	Memoir 1	Memoir 2
Title		
Author		
Memory/ Event/ Relationship		
Lesson Learned		
Rating	_______ /4 stars	_______ /4 stars
What Was Done Well		
What Could Use More Work		

HANDOUT 12.2

FORMATIVE ASSESSMENT 4

Directions: Answer the following questions as best as you can.

1. What is first-person point of view? Give an example sentence.

2. What is third-person point of view? Give an example sentence.

3. Select one of the memoirs read in class.
   a. Which memoir did you pick?

   b. What did you learn about the memoirist in this story?

   c. What are some of his or her character traits?

   d. What textual evidence supports your interpretation of his or her character traits?

HANDOUT 12.2, CONTINUED

4. Add quotation marks to the dialogue below.
   a. Oh no! He yelled. I forgot to bring my sneakers to football practice!
   b. She frowned at him. Please raise your hand before calling out, she said.
   c. Sandy had never been so happy: I can't wait to show you my spelling grade!
5. Read the story below. Take on the role of one of the characters in the story and write a diary entry illustrating that character's reaction to the events. Remember to use first person!

Mandy was sitting in class, listening to her teacher, Dr. Jones talk about habitats. Suddenly, she felt a tug on her long, brown hair. "Ouch!" She said, and turned around. Billy was sitting there with a red face and pink chewing gum on his cheeks. "I blew a bubble with my gum, and some got in your hair," he said. Mandy put her hand on the back of her head and felt the sticky, slimy stuff. She began to wail. Mr. Jones stopped talking and came over to investigate. "What is going on here?" he asked.

LESSON

13 Writing Workshop: Prewriting and First Drafts

MATERIALS

- ✓ Green, red, and yellow cups or index cards (one set per student)
- ✓ Clothespin labeled with student's name (one per student)
- ✓ Index cards (one per student)
- ✓ Handout 13.1: Memoir Museum Parent Letter
- ✓ Handout 13.2: Memoir Map
- ✓ Appendix B10: Class Workshop Chart

- Perspective and purpose affect how we write and how we read the work of others.
- We understand ourselves better when we work to make sense of our own experiences and the experiences of others.

OBJECTIVES

Students will:

- ✓ write interesting story beginnings and endings, and
- ✓ draft, revise, edit, and publish a memoir.

- Prewriting
- First draft
- Revising
- Editing
- Final draft

SEQUENCE

WARM UP

1. Welcome students to their first day of writing workshop. Over the next few lessons, students will use the knowledge they have learned about

nonfiction throughout the unit to create their very own memoir. This story will be published in a class anthology and students will have the opportunity to share an excerpt or highlight from their story at the Memoir Museum for a live audience.

2. Distribute Handout 13.1: Memoir Museum Parent Letter for students to take home. Review the letter with the class and answer any questions students may have. Encourage students to share this letter with their parents, family, or guardians.

INSTRUCTION: SETTING THE SCENE

3. Remind students that well-written stories begin with a hook that grabs readers' attention and makes them want to continue reading. Memoirs do something similar. Memoirists set the scene for the story using a lead that helps the reader picture the setting and visualize what is happening.
4. Share with students some common story beginnings, and ask for examples of each. For example, introductions that:
   - ✓ sound as if writing is a chore (My teacher told us we had to write about . . .),
   - ✓ begin by stating the obvious (This is the beginning of my story . . .),
   - ✓ do not allow the story to unfold naturally (Hello, today I'm going to tell you a story about . . .),
   - ✓ do not introduce characters naturally (My is . . . and I'm writing about . . .), and
   - ✓ are canned or cliché (Once upon a time . . .).

5. Ask: *What do you think of these story beginnings? Do they make you want to continue reading? Are you hooked?*
6. Review some of the introductions of stories students have read during the unit. Ask: *What do you think of these beginnings? Do they set the scene? Do they help the reader visualize what is happening? Do they hook the reader?* As a class, make a list of suggestions for compelling story beginnings.
7. Ask students to think about the memoir they want to write. Have students write an introduction for their memoir in their journals. Allow students to share their beginnings with a shoulder partner.

INSTRUCTION: WRITING WORKSHOP

8. Distribute cups (or cards) and clothespins to students. Tell students:
   - ✓ the green cup means you are busy writing;
   - ✓ the yellow cup means you think you can keep writing, but you have a question and need a teacher conference; and

✓ the red cup means you are stuck and cannot continue writing without some help.

9. Display Appendix B10: Class Workshop Chart. Remind students that writers go through a process when they write. They begin with *prewriting* and then move on to the *first draft*, then *revising*, then *editing*, and, at last, the *final draft*. Add these to the word wall. Remind students that as they go through the stages of the writing process, they should move their clothespin on the chart so that the teacher can monitor the class's progress.

ACTIVITY: WRITING WORKSHOP

10. Begin the writing workshop. Distribute Handout 13.2: Memoir Map. Encourage students to use the map to organize their thoughts and ideas. Monitor student progress through the Class Workshop Chart, and assist students as needed.

2E

- For students who struggle with self-regulation or attention, help students set goals for their work. Consider setting a whole-class goal for everyone to be at a specific stage in the writing process by the end of class, or individual goals according to student needs, which can be written on an index card and taped to students' desks for reference.

- Emphasize that all students work at their own pace: Some writing stages may take some students longer than others. If there are some students who struggle, pull small groups to a back table, or work with individual groups throughout the memoir writing process.

PREPARATION: FOR NEXT LESSON

11. Distribute an index card to each student. Have them write their name on one side and their goal for the next lesson on the other side. Ask students to leave their journals/drafts and index cards on their desks for you to review.
12. Review each student's working drafts and index cards to assess which students are on track and which may be struggling and in need of individual writing conferences or extra guidance during the next few lessons.

- Leave notes for students on their drafts, including suggestions for revision, specific feedback, encouragement, constructive comments, etc.
- If students appear to be struggling, hold individual conferences with them during the next lesson.

HANDOUT 13.1

MEMOIR MUSEUM PARENT LETTER

Dear Parents/Guardians,

Our class has been hard at work learning all about nonfiction and how to write a memoir! We are planning a Memoir Museum in which students will showcase what they have learned by writing a memoir for our class book. They will also share an excerpt or highlight from their memoir for an audience. Students will be writing about a **memory** they have, an **important event**, or a **relationship** they have to a special person, place, or thing.

All work for the Memoir Museum will be completed in class. However, students will bring home progress cards to remind them of what they need to accomplish during the next lesson. Feel free to use these cards as talking points to provide support and guidance to your child on the project.

Your child will bring home a copy of the excerpt he or she wrote in class. Prior to the scheduled presentation at the Memoir Museum, you might help by being an audience as your child practices the planned presentation. Encourage your child to practice reading using a clear, loud voice with appropriate expression. Students do not need to memorize their excerpt.

On the day of the Memoir Museum, encourage your child to think about how he or she could dress to look professional and neat for the presentation. You, your family, and friends are all invited to attend the Memoir Museum, and to celebrate the hard work and growth of our students.

The museum will take place on ______________________ from ______________________. Thank you for your support, we look forward to sharing our memoirs with you!

Sincerely,

HANDOUT 13.2

MEMOIR MAP

Directions: Use this chart to organize your ideas as you work on your memoir.

Title		
Memory/Event/ Relationship	**Setting**	**Other Characters**
Emotional Journey		
Physical/Environmental Details		
1.		
2.		
3.		
4.		
Sensory Details		
1.		
2.		
3.		
4.		
Theme or Lesson Learned		

LESSON

14 Writing Workshop: Revising and Editing

MATERIALS

- ✓ Colored pencils/crayons (class set)
- ✓ Index card (one per student)

- Perspective and purpose affect how we write and how we read the work of others.
- Experience shapes identity.
- Unique points of view are shaped by unique life experiences.
- We understand ourselves better when we work to make sense of our own experiences and the experiences of others.

OBJECTIVES

Students will:

- ✓ write interesting story beginnings and endings, and
- ✓ draft, revise, edit, and publish a memoir.

- Revising
- Editing
- Cover
- Title page
- Dedication
- Biography

SEQUENCE

WARM UP

1. Have students read over the comments on their drafts and review their goal for the day. As students complete tasks during the writing workshop, they should move their clothespins on the Class Writing Chart order to monitor their progress.

ACTIVITY: WRITING WORKSHOP

2. Have students continue to work on their memoirs. Remind students that successful writers continuously revise and edit their work.
3. As students come to a stopping point after revising and editing their memoirs, remind students that the Student Memoir Anthology will contain their memoirs and information about the author. Tell them that, like memoirists, they will also create a cover, title page, sentence-long dedication, and paragraph-long biography about themselves. Add these words to the word wall.
4. Tell students that their biography should only be about a paragraph long and written in third person. Their biographies should contain information that will help readers connect to their memoir. Provide crayons or colored pencils and ask students to be creative when creating the cover for their memoir. However, be sure that students do not get too focused on drawing the cover at the expense of adequately revising and editing their memoirs.

INSTRUCTION: WRITING AN ENDING

5. Remind students that in the last lesson, they discussed the importance of setting the scene of a memoir by writing interesting beginnings. Share with students some common story endings, and ask for examples of each. For example, endings that:
   - abruptly stop with no closure or resolution (I can't think of anything else to write about, so that's all, I guess.);
   - take the easy way out to solve conflict (I realized I was dreaming the whole time.);
   - conveniently resolve conflict (The hero swooped in and saved the day!);
   - are overly strange, unexpected, or disconnected from the story (The world ended and everyone turned into zombies!);
   - seem unrealistically perfect (Everything was wonderful and everyone was happy.); and
   - seem unnecessarily tragic (Everyone died.).

6. Ask: *What do you think of these endings? How would you feel if you were the reader and the story ended that way? How can these endings be changed?* Then, have students compare the bad endings to the exemplary memoir endings, and ask: *What do you think of these endings? Why do you think they are better? What is different about them*? As a class, make a list of suggestions for compelling story endings.
7. Have students look at the endings they have written. Remind students that at the end of a memoir, the theme or lesson that was learned is usu-

ally mentioned. Ask: *How does your story end? Did you learn something? Is the theme clear? Does your ending need more detail? Does your story have a strong ending?*

Students who have completed or nearly completed the writing stage can create a rubric rating for good beginnings and good endings for memoirs.

- Leave notes for students on their drafts, including suggestions for revision, specific feedback, encouragement, constructive comments, etc.
- If students appear to be struggling, hold individual conferences with them during the next lesson.

PREPARATION: FOR NEXT LESSON

8. Distribute an index card to each student. Have them write their name on one side and their goal for the next lesson on the other side. Ask students to leave their journals/drafts and index cards on their desks for you to review.
9. Review each student's working drafts and index cards to assess which students are on track and which may be struggling and in need of individual writing conferences or extra guidance during the next few lessons.

LESSON

15 Writing Workshop: Peer Review and Final Drafts

MATERIALS

- ✓ Yellow, pink, and green sticky notes
- ✓ Index cards
- ✓ Handout 15.1: Memoir Writing Rubric
- ✓ Handout 15.2: Student Performance Checklist

- Perspective and purpose affect how we write and how we read the work of others.
- We understand ourselves better when we work to make sense of our own experiences and the experiences of others.

OBJECTIVES

Students will:

- ✓ evaluate the quality of a memoir using specific characteristics of that genre, and
- ✓ draft, revise, edit, and publish a memoir.

- Peer review

SEQUENCE

WARM UP

1. Display and read aloud the following quote by Sue Monk Kidd: "Stories have to be told or they die, and when they die, we can't remember who we are or why we're here."

2. Ask students to turn to a shoulder partner and discuss: *What does this quote mean? What does the author mean when she says that stories die? Why would this cause us to forget who we are?* Allow for discussion.
3. Have students read over the comments on their drafts and review their goal for the day. As students complete tasks during the writing workshop, they should move their clothespins on the Class Writing Chart order to monitor their progress.

ACTIVITY: PEER REVIEW

4. Pair students by readiness according to Formative Assessment 4. This will help ensure that students of similar writing levels are working together. Ask each pair to find a space in the room with their revised memoir drafts. Distribute Handout 15.1: Memoir Writing Rubric and a stack of sticky notes to each student.
5. Have pairs engage in *peer review*. Add this phrase to the word wall. Encourage students to read their classmate's revised draft twice. The first time, the student should simply read for enjoyment, appreciating the story and becoming familiar with it. The second time, the student should use sticky notes to write comments to the writer:
   - ✓ **Yellow:** Improving sentence variety or correcting mechanics.
   - ✓ **Pink:** Feedback to make the story stronger or suggestions for stronger words/imagery.
   - ✓ **Green:** Positive or encouraging comments about what the other does well.

> During peer review, encourage students to be thoughtful and specific in their feedback. Remind students that peer review should not be overly critical, but should provide information that supports peers in improving their writing. As necessary, model appropriate peer review comments. Encourage each writer to carefully consider all feedback and to determine which advice they will incorporate and which advice they will not.

6. Then, students should score their partner's memoir with Handout 15.1. Partners should take turns explaining comments, feedback, and scoring, and answering any questions that may arise with their classmates once they have finished scoring.

ACTIVITY: WRITING WORKSHOP

7. Have students complete final revisions based on peer review. Students should staple their partner's completed Memoir Writing Rubric to the revised copy of the memoir. Then, students should write their final draft that will be submitted to the class's Memoir Anthology. Remind students they should include a cover, title page, dedication, and biography.
8. As students complete their final drafts, they should review the Memoir Writing Rubric. Emphasize to students that their goal here is to be writing a memoir that receives the highest possible rating in each category.

2E Decide if you would like students to print their final drafts in their neatest handwriting or type them on the computer. Students who struggle with written expression should have the option to use a computer or to dictate to someone who can print or type the memoirs.

9. Distribute Handout 15.2: Student Performance Checklist. Explain how students will be assessed during their presentations. Encourage students to use this checklist to help them prepare for sharing the excerpt from their stories.
10. Have students review their written memoirs and highlight the section of the text that they would like to use as an excerpt during the Memoir Museum.

Consider allowing students who finish early to work on a Memoir Museum program/map for audience members to locate projects throughout the room. They can even use a camera take photos of each student for the program.

PREPARATION: FOR NEXT LESSON

11. Have students neatly turn in all of their completed materials, including their journals.
12. Distribute index cards and have students to write their names on one side. On the other side, ask students to write what they need to do to prepare for the Memoir Museum (e.g., what they plan to wear, how they plan to practice their story excerpt, etc.). Ask: *Do you have all of the pieces needed for your entry in the Memoir Anthology? Did you turn in your performance checklist? Did you turn in your writing rubric? Do you know what you are wearing tomorrow? Do you have the excerpt you picked to read from your memoir so that you can practice it a few times tonight?*
13. Prepare for the Memoir Museum (collect all materials, print the Memoir Anthology and Memoir Museum program/map, and set up desks/tables).

HANDOUT 15.1

MEMOIR WRITING RUBRIC

Memoir Anthology Rubric	1 Memoirist Needing Retraining	2 Memoirist in Training	3 Amateur Memoirist	4 Professional Memoirist
Focuses on a meaningful memory, event (time period), or relationship.	Story lacks focus and jumps from idea to idea; is not centered on a meaningful memory, event (time period), or relationship.	Has little focus on a meaningful memory, event (time period), or relationship, and does not explain the connection to the memoirist.	Focuses somewhat on a meaningful memory, event (time period), or relationship, but does not adequately explain the connection to the memoirist.	Focuses on a meaningful memory, event (time period), or relationship, and explains and reinforces the connection to the memoirist.
Told from the point of view of the main character/ memoirist.	Story is about someone other than the memoirist, and is not from first-person point of view.	Either the story is not about the memoirist, or the story is not told from first-person point of view.	The story is about the main character/ memoirist, but point of view is inconsistent, alternating between first- and third-person point of view.	The story is about the main character/ memoirist, and is told in first-person point of view.
Closely examines a period of time or single event, supporting the main event with details.	Story is not about a focused time or event, but many larger, unrelated stories or sequences of events.	Story examines a period of time or single event, but does not include detail that gives any meaning and understanding of the event and the author's response.	Story examines a period of time or single event, but lacks sufficient detail to give more than bare bones meaning and understanding of the event and the author's response.	Story examines a period of time or single event, adding ample detail to give full meaning and understanding of the event and the author's response.

HANDOUT 15.1, CONTINUED

Memoir Anthology Rubric	1 Memoirist Needing Retraining	2 Memoirist in Training	3 Amateur Memoirist	4 Professional Memoirist
Draws the reader in with sensory details, images, or descriptions.	Writing includes no sensory details, images, or descriptions	Writing includes at least one sensory detail, image, or description.	Writing includes at least two sensory details, images, or descriptions.	Writing includes at least three sensory details, images, or descriptions.
Makes a point, theme, or teaches the reader a lesson.	A point, theme, or lesson is not included.	A point, theme, or lesson is included, but does not fit the story.	A point, theme, or lesson is included and is accurate to the story but unclear.	A point, theme, or lesson is clear, reinforced and accurate to the story.
Explores the memoirist's speech, thoughts, and emotions through dialogue.	There is no dialogue or inside look at the memoirists' speech, thoughts, or emotions.	Minimally uses dialogue to explore the speech, thoughts, and emotions of the memoirist.	Uses some dialogue to illustrate speech, thoughts, and emotions of the memoirist.	Uses ample dialogue to illustrate speech, thoughts, and emotions of the memoirist.
Uses correct mechanics and writing structure.	The story has many grammar and punctuation mistakes and sentences are not varied.	The story has 4–6 grammar or punctuation mistakes, and sentences lack variety.	The story has 1–3 grammar or punctuation mistakes, and sentence variety is inconsistent.	The story has appropriate grammar, punctuation, and sentence variety.

HANDOUT 15.2

STUDENT PERFORMANCE CHECKLIST

Directions: Complete this checklist as you prepare for the Memoir Museum.

Focuses on a meaningful memory, event (time period), or relationship.	❑ Does my story focus on a meaningful memory, important event, or relationship? ❑ Do I explain my connection to a specific memory, event, or relationship?
Told from the point of view of the main character/ memoirist.	❑ Am I the **main character** of the story? ❑ Do I talk about the story using **first-person point of view** (words like "I," "me," and "we")?
Hooks the reader with sensory details, images, or descriptions.	❑ Do I hook the audience with **sensory** details, images, or descriptions?
Closely examines a period of time or single event, and supports the main event with details.	❑ Does my story closely examine a **period of time** or **single event**? ❑ Do I give **details** about the story's plot without giving away the ending?
Has appropriate, professional appearance.	❑ Am I **dressed** appropriately and **professionally**?
Presents story in an exciting and interesting way.	❑ Am I presenting in an **exciting** and **interesting** way? Am I speaking loudly and clearly?

❑ I have stapled a copy of my memoir to this paper and highlighted the excerpt that I plan to share with the audience at the Memoir Museum.

LESSON 16 Memoir Museum

MATERIALS

- ✓ Memoir Museum Program/Map (for students and audience members)
- ✓ Memoir Anthology (for students and audience members)
- ✓ Student computer access to "Coughing and Strawberry Jam" by Milena A. (available at http://teacher.scholastic.com/writeit/readpoem.asp?id=34&genre=Memoir&Page=1&sortBy=)
- ✓ Handout 15.1: Memoir Writing Rubric
- ✓ Handout 16.1: Summative Assessment Rubric
- ✓ Handout 16.2: Performance Assessment
- ✓ Appendix B10: Performance Assessment Answer Key

- Perspective and purpose affect how we write and how we read the work of others.
- Experience shapes identity.
- Unique points of view are shaped by unique life experiences.
- We understand ourselves better when we work to make sense of our own experiences and the experiences of others.

OBJECTIVES

Students will:

- ✓ present a well-written memoir to an audience using articulate presentation skills.

SEQUENCE

1. Invite parents, family, friends, and additional audience members such as students from other grade levels, teachers, and/or school administrators to attend the Memoir Museum. Encourage audience members

For students who may have difficulty speaking in front of an audience, encourage parents/guardians to review with them beforehand the suggested questions that the audience members may ask them. Have students write each question on an index card and then write a short response on the back of the card. Students can read from the cards or refer to them during the museum as needed.

to visit all of students, who will read the selected excerpts from their memoirs.

2. **Summative assessment:** As students present, circulate through the room. Use Handout 16.1: Summative Assessment Rubric to assess their presentations. Evaluate students' final, written narratives published in the student anthology with Handout 15.1: Memoir Writing Rubric.

PREPARATION: PERFORMANCE ASSESSMENT

3. Administer the Unit 2 Performance Assessment (Handout 16.2) during the next lesson or soon after the Memoir Museum. Students will need computer access to read "Coughing and Strawberry Jam." Use the information from the performance to assess students' growth through the unit (i.e., compare this task to responses on the unit preassessment). An answer key is provided (Appendix B10).

Name: ______________________ Date: ____________

HANDOUT 16.1

SUMMATIVE ASSESSMENT RUBRIC

Memoir Museum Presentation Rubric	1 Presenter Needing Retraining	2 Presenter in Training	3 Amateur Presenter	4 Professional Presenter
Preparation	Is clearly unprepared to speak; fumbles with the reading.	Reads clearly, but does not/ cannot look up from reading to engage audience.	Is somewhat prepared but does not clearly articulate the story in an engaging manner.	Clearly well prepared; can clearly articulate the story to be presented; facile enough with reading to look up at audience.
Appearance	Appearance is sloppy. Clothes are messy and posture is slouched or appears not to care about the presentation.	Appearance is not very neat. Looks not quite together. Sometimes is slouched.	Appearance is neat but does not seem to care about the audience	Appearance is neat and professional. Posture shows respect for the audience.
Presentation	Presentation is uninteresting.	Does not speak in an excited or engaged way. Presentation lacks excitement/ engagement and interest.	Speaks with enthusiasm and/ or engagement. Presentation is somewhat interesting.	Appropriate tone (excitement/ engagement) to hold audience interest. Presentation is interesting.
Speaking	Can hardly hear what the speaker is saying.	Speaks too softly, sometimes mumbles words.	Speaks clearly for nearly all of the presentation, but occasionally mumbles.	All of the presentation is projected clearly to the audience.

HANDOUT 16.2

PERFORMANCE ASSESSMENT

Directions: Read "Coughing and Strawberry Jam" by Milena A. (available at http://teacher.scholastic.com/writeit/readpoem.asp?id=34&genre=Memoir&Page=1&sortBy=). Then, answer the following questions.

1. What is nonfiction?
   a. A true story
   b. A made up story

2. What genre is this story?
   a. Biography
   b. Informational text
   c. Autobiography
   d. Memoir

3. What is the lesson the memoirist learned in this story?
   a. Be kind to others, even when they don't deserve it.
   b. Think before you speak; you can't take back harmful words once they are spoken.
   c. Always tell people that you love them, because you may not be given another chance.
   d. Never judge a book by its cover.

4. Who is the main character and memoirist who is telling this story?
   a. The grandmother
   b. Milena's mom
   c. A third-person narrator
   d. Milena

5. What point of view is this story told from?
   a. First person
   b. Third person

6. Label the following as (I) for internal event or (E) for external event.
   a. _______ "If she tells me to put on a sweater one more time, I'm going to scream!"
   b. _______ "I used to sit on her bed and play cards with her."
   c. _______ "I bit my tongue and would murmur, 'love you.'"
   d. _______ "We are her life, I realized."

HANDOUT 16.2, CONTINUED

7. Which sensory detail is being used in the following sentences? Sight, touch, or smell?
   a. ________________ "As I lay on her bed last night, feeling her shaky movements through the old mattress."
   b. ________________ "Nursing homes and hospitals smelling of rubbing alcohol and death."

8. What is the main idea of this story?
   a. Milena's grandmother annoys her.
   b. Milena's grandmother comes to live with her.
   c. Milena's father doesn't like her grandmother.
   d. We sometimes don't appreciate what we have until it is too late.

9. What character traits would you use to describe Milena at the end of the story?
   a. Selfish and self-centered
   b. Thoughtful and regretful
   c. Rude and close-minded
   d. Trustworthy and smart

10. What relationship or memory does this memoir focus on?
    a. Melina's relationship with her family
    b. Melina's memory of a nursing home.
    c. Melina's relationship with her grandmother.
    d. Melina's memory of family photographs.

References

Blume, J. (2008). *Cool zone with the pain and the great one.* New York, NY: Random House.

Burns, D. E. (1987). *The effects of group training activities on students' creative productivity.* (Unpublished doctoral dissertation). The University of Connecticut, Storrs, CT.

Callahan, C. M., Moon, T. R., Oh, S., & Hailey, E. (2015). Documenting the effects of an integrated curricular/instructional model for gifted students. *American Educational Research Journal, 52,* 137–167.

Chase, J. (2014). *During the reign of the queen of Persia.* New York, NY: New York Review of Books.

Csikszentmihalyi, M. (1990). *Flow: The psychology of optimal experience.* New York, NY: Harper & Row.

Csikszentmihalyi, M., Rathunde, K. R., & Whalen, S. (1993). *Talented teenagers: The roots of success and failure.* New York, NY: Cambridge University Press.

Donovan, M., Bransford, J., & Pellegrino, J. (1999). *How people learn: Bridging research and practice.* Washington, DC: National Academy Press.

Dweck, C. S. (2006). *Mindset: The new psychology of success.* New York, NY: Ballantine Books.

Freire, P. (1970). *Pedagogy of the oppressed* (M. B. Ramos, Trans.). New York, NY: Continuum.

Freire, P., & Macedo, D. (1987). *Literacy: Reading the word and the world.* Westport, CT: Bergin & Garvey.

Howard, P. (1994). *An owner's manual for the brain.* Austin, TX: Leorian Press.

Jensen, E. (1998). *Teaching with the brain in mind.* Alexandria, VA: Association for Supervision & Curriculum Development.

Kaplan, S. (2005). Layering differential curricula for gifted and talented. In F. Karnes & S. Bean (Eds.), *Methods and materials for teaching gifted students* (pp. 107–132). Waco, TX: Prufrock Press.

Kaplan, S. (2013). Depth and complexity. In C. M. Callahan & H. L. Hertberg-Davis (Eds.), *Fundamentals of gifted education* (pp. 277–287). New York, NY: Routledge.

National Association for Gifted Children. (2010). *Pre-K to grade 12 gifted programming standards.* Retrieved from http://www.nagc.org/index.aspx?id=546

National Council of Teachers of English, & International Reading Association. (2012). *Standards for the English language arts.* Urbana, IL: NCTE.

Olenchak, F. R. (1991). Assessing program effects for gifted/learning disabled students. In R. Swassing & A. Robinson (Eds.), *NAGC 1991 research briefs* (pp. 86–89). Washington, DC: National Association for Gifted Children.

Packard, E. (2010). *Return to the cave of time (U-ventures).* New York, NY: Simon & Schuster.

Palacio, R. J. (2012). *Wonder.* New York, NY: Random House.

Reis, S. M. (1981). *An analysis of the productivity of gifted students participating in programs using the revolving door identification model* (Unpublished doctoral dissertation). University of Connecticut, Storrs, CT.

Renzulli, J. S., & Reis, S. (1985). *The schoolwide enrichment model: A comprehensive plan for educational excellence.* Mansfield Center, CT: Creative Learning Press.

Renzulli, J. S., & Reis, S. (2001). The schoolwide enrichment model. In K. A. Heller, F. J. Mönks, R. J. Sternberg, & R. F. Subotnik (Eds.), *International handbook of giftedness and talent* (2nd ed., pp. 367–382). Oxford, England: Elsevier Science, Ltd.

Ransom, I. (2016). Archery: Kim throws down gauntlet with world record. *Reuters.* Retrieved from http://www.reuters.com/article/us-olympics-rio-archery-record-idUSKCN10G1KS

Roach Smith, M. (2014). *Writing lessons: How to access the details for writing memoir.* Retrieved from http://marionroach.com/2014/01/how-to-access-the-details-for-writing

Roberts, L. (2008). Nightmares, idylls, mystery, and hope: *Walk Two Moons* and the artifice of realism in children's fiction. *Children's Literature in Education, 39*, 121–134.

Schack, G. D., Starko, A. J., & Burns, D. E. (1991). Self-efficacy and creative productivity: Three studies of above average ability children. *Journal of Research in Education, 1*, 44–52.

Sousa, D., & Tomlinson, C. (2010). *Differentiation and the brain: How neuroscience supports the learner-friendly classroom*. Bloomington, IN: Solution Tree.

Sternberg, R. J. (1986). A triarchic theory of intellectual giftedness. In R. J. Sternberg & J. E. Davidson (Eds.), *Conceptions of giftedness* (pp. 223–243). New York, NY: Cambridge University Press.

Tomlinson, C. A. (1995). *How to differentiate instruction in mixed-ability classrooms*. Alexandria, VA: Association for Supervision and Curriculum Development.

Tomlinson, C. A. (1999). *The differentiated classroom: Responding to the needs of all learners*. Alexandria, VA: Association for Supervision and Curriculum Development.

Wenglinsky, H. (2002). How schools matter: The link between teacher classroom practices and student academic performance. *Education Policy Analysis Archives, 10* (12). Retrieved from http://epaa.asu.edu/ojs/article/view/291

Williams, T. (1999). *The glass menagerie*. New York, NY: New Directions. (Original work published 1945)

Appendices
Unit Resources

APPENDIX A1

ROAD TO PUBLISHING: IMAGERY AND SETTING

Your editor says...

Element	You need to go back to the drawing board . . .	You need multiple revisions . . .	You need one more revision . . .	Your work is publishable!
Imagery	There is no imagery.	The imagery is confusing and does not seem related to story elements.	The imagery does not always fit with the other story elements.	The imagery fits well with the other story elements.
Setting	The setting is never clarified.	There are missing details about the setting without a reason.	Some details of the setting are inconsistent.	The setting is clear and consistent.

APPENDIX A2

ROAD TO PUBLISHING: CHARACTERS

Your editor says...

Element	You need to go back to the drawing board . . .	You need multiple revisions . . .	You need one more revision . . .	Your work is publishable!
Characters (*Note.* Stock characters are not required.)	There are no characters developed enough to be a protagonist/antagonist/stock character.	The protagonist/antagonist are underdeveloped. The stock character serves no purpose.	The protagonist/antagonist are identifiable. The stock character has a debatable purpose.	The protagonist/antagonist are well-developed. The stock character serves a clear purpose.

APPENDIX A3

ROAD TO PUBLISHING: CHARACTERIZATION

Your editor says...

Element	You need to go back to the drawing board . . .	You need multiple revisions . . .	You need one more revision . . .	Your work is publishable!
Characterization	Either direct or indirect characterization is missing.	There is an uneven balance between direct and indirect characterization that is distracting to the reader.	The direct and/or indirect characterization is developed but inconsistent.	Both direct and indirect characterization is consistent and well-developed.

APPENDIX A4

ROAD TO PUBLISHING: DIALOGUE

Your editor says...

Element	You need to go back to the drawing board . . .	You need multiple revisions . . .	You need one more revision . . .	Your work is publishable!
Dialogue	There is no dialogue, even when it would be relevant.	There is dialogue, but there are issues with punctuation and/or flow (e.g., it is difficult to tell who is speaking).	The dialogue does not seem authentic to the characters.	The dialogue flows well and is authentic to the characters.

APPENDIX A5

ROAD TO PUBLISHING: POINT OF VIEW

Your editor says...

Element	You need to go back to the drawing board . . .	You need multiple revisions . . .	You need one more revision . . .	Your work is publishable!
Point of View	The point of view switches narrators at random.	The point of view is inconsistent and confusing at times.	The point of view is clear, although there are minor issues with consistency.	The point of view is clear and consistent.

APPENDIX A6

ROAD TO PUBLISHING: CONFLICT

Your editor says...

Element	You need to go back to the drawing board . . .	You need multiple revisions . . .	You need one more revision . . .	Your work is publishable!
Conflict	There is no major conflict.	The major conflict is unclear.	The major conflict is identifiable.	The major conflict is clearly identifiable and well-developed.

APPENDIX A7
WRITING PROMPT BANK

Directions: Select a prompt for each student based on any weaknesses noted in students' writing during Formative Assessment 3. If no weaknesses are noted, have the student select their own preferred prompt based on what they perceive is an area to work on developing.

CHARACTERIZATION

- Describe an action so it reveals something significant about the character who does it (500 word max).
- Write interior monologues for five different characters with different feelings (sadness, anger, joy, jealousy, boredom), who are all at recess (100 words each).

CONFLICT

- Describe one conflict in three different ways (wonderful, sad, scary; 100 words each).
- Write a dialogue where two people argue about something unimportant, but the argument reveals an important conflict between the two.

DIALOGUE

- Write a dialogue between two characters in which one character says something other than what he or she is thinking. Use actions or gestures to reveal this character's actual meaning (one page max).

IMAGERY

- Make an extraordinary event sound ordinary (500 word max).
- Describe two people eating a meal without dialogue (500 word max).
- Describe an event witnessed by an unreliable narrator, which indirectly conveys what is actually happening (500 word max).
- Using only sensory details, describe a person so it is clear the narrator has a negative attitude toward the person.
- Using only sensory details, describe a person so a good feeling toward the person is evident.

POINT OF VIEW

- Describe a character (observed) from the point of view of another character (observer), but the description should reveal more about the observer than the observed—this should be in first person.
- Describe a character (observed) from the point of view of another character (observer), but the description should reveal more about the observer than the observed—this should be in third person.

APPENDIX A8

ROAD TO PUBLISHING: PLOT

Your editor says...

Element	You need to go back to the drawing board . . .	You need multiple revisions . . .	You need one more revision . . .	Your work is publishable!
Plot	The plot is hard to follow.	There are gaps in the plot.	There are minor points of confusion in the plot.	The plot is clear and easy to follow.

APPENDIX B1

FORMATIVE ASSESSMENT 1 ANSWER KEY

1.
   a. Paragraph 2.
   b. "Very superior," "best training in the world," "well-deserved accolades," "untouchable prowess," "poor judges at this event."

2.
   a. Description 2.
   b. First-person point of view tells the story from the author's perspective using "I," "me," "we," etc. Third-person point of view tells the story as someone observing an event or person using people's names and pronouns like "he," "she," they," "them," etc.

APPENDIX B2

BIOGRAPHY VERSUS AUTOBIOGRAPHY ANSWER KEY

1. Autobiography
2. Biography
3. Autobiography
4. Biography
5. Autobiography
6. Biography
7. Both
8. Both
9. Both
10. Both
11. Both
12. Both

APPENDIX B3

FORMATIVE ASSESSMENT 2 ANSWER KEY

1. Writing that is based on fact and/or memory. Characters and settings are real.
2. A personal story that reflects a person's memory of an event or a time period, a relationship, etc. Events are told in first person by the person who experienced the event(s).
3. The story of a person written from birth to death or a particular time period by another person based on facts and documentation.
4.
   a. M
   b. B
   c. B
   d. M

5. Informational texts provided descriptions of events or how to carry out a task (e.g., news, directions), while biography is the story of a person's life or some significant portion of that person's life. Both are based on fact and documentation of those facts.
6. An autobiography is the story of a person's life told from that person's perspective. Autobiographies are also supposed to be based on fact and documentation of those facts.

APPENDIX B4

FOCUS ON THE RUBRIC, PART 1

Memoir Anthology Rubric	1 Memoirist Needing Retraining	2 Memoirist in Training	3 Amateur Memoirist	4 Professional Memoirist
Focuses on a meaningful memory, event (time period), or relationship.	Story lacks focus and jumps from idea to idea; is not centered on a meaningful memory, event (time period), or relationship.	Has little focus on a meaningful memory, event (time period), or relationship, and does not explain the connection to the memoirist.	Focuses somewhat on a meaningful memory, event (time period), or relationship, but does not adequately explain the connection to the memoirist.	Focuses on a meaningful memory, event (time period), or relationship, and explains and reinforces the connection to the memoirist.
Told from the point of view of the main character/ memoirist.	Story is about someone other than the memoirist, and is not from first-person point of view.	Either the story is not about the memoirist, or the story is not told from first-person point of view.	The story is about the main character/ memoirist, but point of view is inconsistent, alternating between first- and third-person point of view.	The story is about the main character/ memoirist, and is told in first-person point of view.

APPENDIX B5

FOCUS ON THE RUBRIC, PART 2

Memoir Anthology Rubric	1 Memoirist Needing Retraining	2 Memoirist in Training	3 Amateur Memoirist	4 Professional Memoirist
Closely examines a period of time or single event, supporting the main event with details.	Story is not about a focused time or event, but many larger, unrelated stories or sequences of events.	Story examines a period of time or single event, but does not include detail that gives any meaning and understanding of the event and the author's response.	Story examines a period of time or single event, but lacks sufficient detail to give more than bare bones meaning and understanding of the event and the author's response.	Story examines a period of time or single event, adding ample detail to give full meaning and understanding of the event and the author's response.

APPENDIX B6

FOCUS ON THE RUBRIC, PART 3

Memoir Anthology Rubric	1 Memoirist Needing Retraining	2 Memoirist in Training	3 Amateur Memoirist	4 Professional Memoirist
Draws the reader in with sensory details, images, or descriptions.	Writing includes no sensory details, images, or descriptions	Writing includes at least one sensory detail, image, or description.	Writing includes at least two sensory details, images, or descriptions.	Writing includes at least three sensory details, images, or descriptions.

APPENDIX B7

FOCUS ON THE RUBRIC, PART 4

Memoir Anthology Rubric	1 Memoirist Needing Retraining	2 Memoirist in Training	3 Amateur Memoirist	4 Professional Memoirist
Makes a point, theme, or teaches the reader a lesson.	A point, theme, or lesson is not included.	A point, theme, or lesson is included, but does not fit the story.	A point, theme, or lesson is included and is accurate to the story but unclear.	A point, theme, or lesson is clear, reinforced and accurate to the story.

APPENDIX B8

FOCUS ON THE RUBRIC, PART 5

Memoir Anthology Rubric	1 Memoirist Needing Retraining	2 Memoirist in Training	3 Amateur Memoirist	4 Professional Memoirist
Explores the memoirist's speech, thoughts, and emotions through dialogue.	There is no dialogue or inside look at the memoirists' speech, thoughts, or emotions.	Minimally uses dialogue to explore the speech, thoughts, and emotions of the memoirist.	Uses some dialogue to illustrate speech, thoughts, and emotions of the memoirist.	Uses ample dialogue to illustrate speech, thoughts, and emotions of the memoirist.
Uses correct mechanics and writing structure.	The story has many grammar and punctuation mistakes and sentences are not varied.	The story has 4–6 grammar or punctuation mistakes, and sentences lack variety.	The story has 1–3 grammar or punctuation mistakes, and sentence variety is inconsistent.	The story has appropriate grammar, punctuation, and sentence variety.

APPENDIX B9

CLASS WORKSHOP CHART

Where Are You in the Writing Process?
Final Draft
Editing
Revising
First Draft
Prewriting

APPENDIX B10

PERFORMANCE ASSESSMENT ANSWER KEY

1. A
2. D
3. C
4. D
5. A
6. I, E, E, I
7. Touch, smell
8. D
9. B
10. C

About the Authors

Carolyn M. Callahan, Ph.D., Commonwealth Professor of Education at the University of Virginia, developed and leads the master's and doctoral programs in gifted education, teaches classes in gifted education, and developed the summer and Saturday enrichment programs at UVA. For 20 years she has been the principal investigator on projects of the National Research Center on the Gifted and Talented (NRC/GT), and she has been principal investigator on five Javits grants. Her work with the NRC/GT and with the Javits projects has focused on curriculum development and implementation. As part of her work with the NRC/GT she was coevaluator for the U.S. Department of Education of the Javits program and conducted a national survey of gifted and talented programs. She has conducted evaluations of grant projects including several Javits grants, state-level programs (e.g., the Advanced Placement initiative in Maine), and local-level gifted programs large and small. She has been recognized as Outstanding Professor of the Commonwealth of Virginia and Distinguished Scholar of the National Association for Gifted Children (NAGC). She has served as president of NAGC and the Association for the Gifted, and as editor of *Gifted Child Quarterly*. Dr. Callahan has published more than 200 articles and 50 book chapters on topics in gifted education with one of those publications considered the definitive book on evaluation. She is the coeditor of the recently published books, *Fundamentals of Gifted Education: Considering Multiple Perspectives* and *Critical Issues in Gifted Education.*

Tracy C. Missett, Ph.D., is an assistant professor at the University of Montana Phyllis J. Washington College of Education and Human Sciences, where she holds the Suzanne and Dave Peterson Endowed Professorship in Gifted Education. Dr. Missett received her Ph.D. and B.A. from the University of Virginia, her J.D. from the University of California, Hastings College of the Law, and her M.A. from Teachers College, Columbia University. While a doctoral student at the University of Virginia, Dr. Missett was a Graduate Research Assistant on a project of the National Research Center on the Gifted and Talented (NRC/GT) and engaged in research on the effectiveness of the CLEAR Curriculum Model. Dr. Missett has published multiple articles and book chapters on topics in gifted education, and she has received awards in both curriculum and research from the National Association for Gifted Children.

Amy Price Azano, Ph.D., is an assistant professor of adolescent literacy at Virginia Tech where her research focuses on rural gifted education, place-based pedagogy, and the literacy needs of rural youth. Dr. Azano teaches graduate-level literacy courses to preservice teachers and doctoral students and serves as coprincipal investigator on a 5-year, Jacob K. Javits Department of Education grant seeking to improve gifted education for rural learners. She is also an affiliate faculty member, leading the education research core, with the Virginia Tech Center for Autism Research, and does extensive community outreach in the field of autism. Prior to her current position, Dr. Azano was a researcher and project manager on the "What Works in Gifted Education" study at the National Research Center on the Gifted and Talented (NRC/GT) at the University of Virginia (UVA). Before earning her Ph.D. in English Education from UVA, Dr. Azano taught high school English and served as codirector of UVA's National Writing Project site. Her recent publications can be found in *American Educational Research Journal, English Education, Journal of Advanced Academics, Journal of Research in Rural Education, Journal of Teaching Writing,* and *Teaching Exceptional Children.*

Melanie Caughey is a Graduate Research Assistant at the University of Virginia, where she is completing her Ph.D. She worked on adapting the CLEAR Curriculum Model for the Javits project Promoting PLACE in Rural Schools. Ms. Caughey also serves as the Academic Coordinator for the Saturday and Summer Enrichment Programs (SEP) and has worked with the National Center for Research on Gifted Education (NCRGE). She received her B.A. in English and Education from Bucknell University and her M.S. in Educational Studies from Duquesne University. Prior to coming to UVA, Ms. Caughey taught Advanced Placement (AP) English Literature, dual enrollment college composition, public speaking, journalism, and senior English in Ligonier, PA. She has presented her research on AP and dual enrollment coursework, differentiating in AP courses, and AP/gifted education policy, as well as her work with Promoting PLACE/the NCRGE, at numerous conferences throughout the U.S.

Annalissa V. Brodersen, Ph.D., is a Research Associate with the National Center for Research on Gifted Education and Project PLACE at the University of Virginia. Prior to her graduate work, she served as a project coordinator on the Family Transitions Project at Iowa State University. Her research interests include Pre-K–12 gifted education policies and practices, rural education, and intersections between Pre-K–12 gifted education and higher education. More specifically, her current work examines challenges to implementing gifted education policy in a variety of school settings, including rural, low-income schools. Her teaching interests are in broadening perspectives of giftedness based on psychological and educational theory, student development in emerging adulthood, and theoretically sound assessment practices. She currently teaches an introductory course in gifted education at the University of Virginia.

Mary Tackett, Ph.D., an Assistant Professor of Education at Sweet Briar College in Virginia, specializes in elementary education and reading instruction. Her research interests focus on underserved, culturally diverse learners and special populations within the context of reading and literacy, and she specifically focuses on how teachers can utilize diverse children's books within classroom contexts to address salient societal issues. Dr. Tackett earned her Ph.D. in Curriculum and Instruction at Virginia Tech where she was named the 2016 Graduate Student of the Year. During her time at Virginia Tech, where she also earned her bachelor's, master's, and reading specialist degrees, she worked as a Graduate Research Assistant on the Jacob K. Javits grant, "Promoting PLACE in Rural Schools," funded by the U.S. Department of Education. Prior to her career as a teacher educator, she taught first, second, and fifth grade, and has also engaged in teacher preparation and supervision, literacy coaching, curriculum development, and reading and writing instruction and intervention at the primary, secondary, and collegiate levels.

Common Core State Standards Alignment

Domain	Grade 4 ELA-Literacy Common Core State Standards
Reading: Literature	RL.4.1 Refer to details and examples in a text when explaining what the text says explicitly and when drawing inferences from the text.
	RL.4.2 Determine a theme of a story, drama, or poem from details in the text; summarize the text.
	RL.4.3 Describe in depth a character, setting, or event in a story or drama, drawing on specific details in the text (e.g., a character's thoughts, words, or actions).
	RL.4.4 Determine the meaning of words and phrases as they are used in a text, including those that allude to significant characters found in mythology (e.g., Herculean).
	RL.4.5 Explain major differences between poems, drama, and prose, and refer to the structural elements of poems (e.g., verse, rhythm, meter) and drama (e.g., casts of characters, settings, descriptions, dialogue, stage directions) when writing or speaking about a text.
	RL.4.6 Compare and contrast the point of view from which different stories are narrated, including the difference between first- and third-person narrations.
	RL.4.7 Make connections between the text of a story or drama and a visual or oral presentation of the text, identifying where each version reflects specific descriptions and directions in the text.

Domain	Grade 4 ELA-Literacy Common Core State Standards
Reading: Literature, *continued*	RL.4.9 Compare and contrast the treatment of similar themes and topics (e.g., opposition of good and evil) and patterns of events (e.g., the quest) in stories, myths, and traditional literature from different cultures.
	RL.4.10 By the end of the year, read and comprehend literature, including stories, dramas, and poetry, in the grades 4–5 text complexity band proficiently, with scaffolding as needed at the high end of the range.
Writing	W.4.1 Write opinion pieces on topics or texts, supporting a point of view with reasons and information.
	W.4.2 Write informative/explanatory texts to examine a topic and convey ideas and information clearly.
	W.4.3 Write narratives to develop real or imagined experiences or events using effective technique, descriptive details, and clear event sequences.
	W.4.4 Produce clear and coherent writing in which the development and organization are appropriate to task, purpose, and audience.
	W.4.5 With guidance and support from peers and adults, develop and strengthen writing as needed by planning, revising, and editing.
	W.4.6 With some guidance and support from adults, use technology, including the Internet, to produce and publish writing as well as to interact and collaborate with others; demonstrate sufficient command of keyboarding skills to type a minimum of one page in a single sitting.
	W.4.7 Conduct short research projects that build knowledge through investigation of different aspects of a topic.
	W.4.8 Recall relevant information from experiences or gather relevant information from print and digital sources; take notes and categorize information, and provide a list of sources.
	W.4.9 Draw evidence from literary or informational texts to support analysis, reflection, and research.
	W.4.10 Write routinely over extended time frames (time for research, reflection, and revision) and shorter time frames (a single sitting or a day or two) for a range of discipline-specific tasks, purposes, and audiences.